Contents

Introduction *1*

Part 1 The control of legionella bacteria in evaporative cooling systems *7*

Evaporative cooling systems: Types, design and operation *9*

Requirements of a cooling water treatment programme *17*

Inspection, cleaning and disinfection procedures *27*

Monitoring water quality and understanding water treatment analytical reports *41*

Part 2 The control of bacteria in hot and cold water systems *49*

Types and application of hot and cold water systems *51*

Water system design and commissioning *61*

Operation and inspection of hot and cold water systems *68*

Water treatment and control programmes for hot and cold water systems *77*

Microbiological monitoring *83*

Cleaning and disinfection *85*

Shared premises and residential accommodation: Landlords *88*

Special considerations for healthcare and care homes *91*

Part 3 The control of legionella bacteria in other risk systems   97

Introduction   99

What are other risk systems?   99

Risk identification and control   100

Appendices

1 Legionella risk assessment   102

2 Legionella written control scheme   104

3 Action in the event of an outbreak of legionellosis   105

4 Example of sentinel points in a simple hot water system (HWS)   106

5 Example of sentinel points in a complex hot water system (HWS)   107

6 Checklist for recommended frequency of inspection for other risk systems   108

References   111

Glossary   114

Further sources of advice   119

Acknowledgements   119

Further information   120

Introduction

1   This guidance is for dutyholders, which includes employers, those in control of premises and those with health and safety responsibilities for others, to help them comply with their legal duties. It gives practical guidance on how to assess and control the risks due to legionella bacteria.

2   Any water system that has the right environmental conditions could potentially be a source for legionella bacteria growth. There is a reasonably foreseeable legionella risk in your water system if:

- water is stored or re-circulated as part of your system;
- the water temperature in all or some part of the system may be between 20–45 °C;
- there are deposits that can support bacterial growth, such as rust, sludge, scale and organic matter;
- it is possible for water droplets to be produced and, if so, if they can be dispersed;
- it is likely that any of your employees, contractors, visitors etc could be exposed to any contaminated water droplets.

Health and safety law

3   *Legionnaires' disease: The control of legionella bacteria in water systems. Approved Code of Practice*[1] gives specific information on the health and safety law that applies. In brief, general duties under the Health and Safety at Work etc Act 1974 (the HSW Act)[2] extend to risks from legionella bacteria, which may arise from work activities. The Management of Health and Safety at Work Regulations 1999 provide a broad framework for controlling health and safety at work (see www.hse.gov.uk/risk for more information). More specifically, the Control of Substances Hazardous to Health Regulations 2002 (COSHH)[3] provide a framework of duties designed to assess, prevent or control the risks from hazardous substances, including biological agents such as legionella, and take suitable precautions.

4   The essential elements of COSHH are:

- risk assessment;
- prevention of exposure or substitution with a less hazardous substance if this is possible, or substitute a process or method with a less hazardous one;
- control of exposure where prevention or substitution is not reasonably practicable;
- maintenance, examination and testing of control measures, eg automatic dosing equipment for delivery of biocides and other treatment chemicals;
- provision of information, instruction and training for employees;
- health surveillance of employees (where appropriate, and if there are valid techniques for detecting indications of disease) where exposure may result in an identifiable disease or adverse health effect.

5   Under general health and safety law, dutyholders including employers or those in control of premises, must ensure the health and safety of their employees or others who may be affected by their undertaking. They must take suitable precautions to prevent or control the risk of exposure to legionella. They also need to either understand, or appoint somebody competent who knows how to identify and assess sources of risk, manage those risks, prevent or control any risks, keep records and carry out any other legal duties they may have.

Other relevant legislation

6   Employers must be aware of other legislation they may need to comply with, which includes the Notification of Cooling Towers and Evaporative Condensers Regulations 1992;[4] Reporting of Injuries, Diseases and Dangerous Occurrences Regulations 2013 (RIDDOR);[5] the Safety Representatives and Safety Committees Regulations 1977 and the Health and Safety (Consultation with Employees) Regulations 1996.[6]

Notification of Cooling Towers and Evaporative Condensers Regulations 1992

7   These Regulations require employers to notify the local authority, in writing, if they operate a cooling tower or evaporative condenser and include details about where they are located. The Regulations also require notification when such devices are no longer in use. Notification forms are available from your local environmental health department.

Reporting of Injuries, Diseases and Dangerous Occurrences Regulations 2013 (RIDDOR)

8   These regulations require employers and those in control of premises to report accidents and some diseases that arise out of or in connection with work to HSE. Cases of legionellosis are reportable under RIDDOR if a medical practitioner notifies the employer; and the employee's current job involves work on or near cooling systems that are located in the workplace and use water; or work on water service systems located in the workplace, which are likely to be a source of contamination. For more information, see HSE guidance at www.hse.gov.uk/riddor/index.htm.

The Safety Representatives and Safety Committees Regulations 1977 and the Health and Safety (Consultation with Employees) Regulations 1996

9   These regulations require employers to consult trade union safety representatives, other employee representatives, or employees where there are no representatives, about health and safety matters. This includes changes to the work that may affect their health and safety, arrangements for getting competent help, information on the risks and controls, and the planning of health and safety training.

Identify and assess sources of risk

10   Carrying out a legionella risk assessment and ensuring it remains up to date is required under health and safety law and is a key duty when managing the risk of exposure to legionella bacteria. In conducting the assessment, the dutyholder must appoint a competent person or persons, known as the responsible person(s), to help them meet their health and safety duties, ie take responsibility for managing the control scheme. If the necessary competence, knowledge and expertise does not exist, there may be a need to appoint someone externally (see paragraphs 16–22).

11   The responsible person(s) appointed to take day-to-day responsibility for managing risks in their business will need to understand the water systems, any equipment associated with the system, and all its constituent parts. They should be able to identify if the water systems are likely to create a risk from exposure to legionella bacteria by assessing if:

- water is stored or re-circulated in the system;
- the water temperature in all or some parts of the system may be between 20–45 °C;
- there are deposits that support bacterial growth, including legionella, such as rust, sludge, scale, organic matter and biofilms;
- it is possible for water droplets to be produced and, if so, whether they can be dispersed;

■   it is likely that any of your employees, contractors, visitors, the public etc could be exposed to contaminated water droplets.

12 The practical risk assessment should include a site survey of all the water systems and consider other health and safety aspects of undertaking such investigations, eg working at height or in confined spaces or the need for permits-to-work when doing this.

13 Appendix 1 provides information on the key requirements when assessing the risks associated with any water systems. Further information is also available in BS 8580 *Water quality. Risk assessments for Legionella control. Code of Practice*[7] and in The Water Management Society's *Guide to risk assessment for water services*.[8] In summary, the risk assessment should consider and evaluate:

■   clear allocation of management responsibilities;
■   competence and training of key personnel;
■   a description of the water system, including an up-to-date schematic diagram;
■   an evaluation of the risk;
■   safe operating procedures for the water system, including controls in place to control risks;
■   monitoring, inspection and maintenance procedures;
■   results of monitoring, inspection and any checks carried out;
■   limitations of the legionella risk assessment;
■   arrangements to review the risk assessment regularly and particularly when there is reason to suspect it is no longer valid.

Info box: Schematic diagram

A schematic diagram is a simplified but accurate illustration of the layout of the water system, including parts temporarily out of use. While providing only an indication of the scale, it is an important tool as it allows any person who is not familiar with the system to understand quickly and easily their layout, without any specialised training or experience. These are not formal technical drawings but show what the systems comprise of, illustrating plant and equipment, including servicing and control valves, any components potentially relevant to the legionella risk, including outlets, strainers and filters or parts that are out of use.

---

14 If the risk assessment concludes there is no reasonably foreseeable risk or the risks are insignificant and are managed properly to comply with the law, the assessment is complete. Although no further action may be required at this stage, existing controls must be maintained. The assessment of risk is an ongoing process and not merely a paper exercise. Dutyholders should arrange to review the assessment regularly and specifically when there is reason to suspect it is no longer valid. An indication of when to review the assessment and what to consider should be recorded and this may result from, eg:

■   a change to the water system or its use;
■   a change to the use of the building where the system is installed;
■   new information available about risks or control measures;
■   the results of checks indicating that control measures are no longer effective;
■   changes to key personnel;
■   a case of legionnaires' disease/legionellosis associated with the system.

15 Communication is a key factor in the risk assessment process. The risk needs to be identified and communicated to management to allow them to prioritise remedial actions to control it.

Managing the risk

16 Inadequate management, lack of training and poor communication can be contributory factors in outbreaks of legionnaires' disease. It is important that those people involved in assessing risk and applying precautions are competent, trained and aware of their responsibilities.

17 The dutyholder should specifically appoint a competent person or persons to take day-to-day responsibility for controlling any identified risk from legionella bacteria. It is important for the appointed person, known as the responsible person(s), to have **sufficient authority, competence and knowledge of the installation** to ensure all operational procedures are carried out in a timely and effective manner.

18 The responsible person(s) appointed to implement the control measures and strategies should be suitably informed, instructed and trained and their suitability assessed. Regular refresher training should be given and the responsible person(s) should have a clear understanding of their role and the overall health and safety management structure and policy in the organisation.

19 If a dutyholder is self-employed or a member of a partnership, and is competent, they may appoint themselves. Many businesses can develop the necessary expertise in house and are well equipped to manage health and safety themselves. However, if there are some things they are not able to do, it is important to get external help. If there are several people responsible for managing risks, eg because of shift-work patterns, the dutyholder needs to make sure that everyone knows what they are responsible for and how they fit into the overall risk management of the system.

20 Identifying and deciding what help is needed is very important but it is the responsibility of the dutyholder to ensure those appointed to carry out the tasks given to them have adequate information and support.

21 Dutyholders can use specialist contractors to undertake aspects of the operation, maintenance and control measures required for their water system. While these contractors have legal responsibilities, the ultimate responsibility for the safe operation of the water system rests with the dutyholder. It is important they are satisfied that any contractors employed are competent to carry out the required tasks and that the tasks are carried out to the required standards. The contractor should inform the dutyholder of any risks identified and how the system can be operated and maintained safely.

22 There are a number of external schemes to help you with this, such as the Legionella Control Association's *A Recommended Code of Conduct for Service Providers*.[9]

Preventing or controlling the risk

23 First, consider whether the risk of legionella can be prevented by considering the type of water systems needed. Where the risk cannot be prevented, a course of action must be devised to manage the risk by implementing effective control measures. The written scheme should be specific and tailored to the systems covered by the risk assessment. Appendix 2 summarises the key information, which should include the following precautions:

- ensuring the release of water spray is properly controlled;
- avoiding conditions that support growth of microorganisms, including legionella;
- ensuring water cannot stagnate anywhere in the system by regular movement

of water in all sections of the systems and by keeping pipe lengths as short as possible, and/or removing redundant pipework and deadlegs;

■ avoiding using materials that harbour bacteria and other microorganisms or provide nutrients for microbial growth (the *Water Fittings and Materials Directory*[10] lists fittings, materials, and appliances approved for use on the UK Water Supply System by the Water Regulations Advisory Scheme. Those approved are tested against BS 6920);[11]

■ keeping the system and the water in it clean;

■ treating water to either control the growth of microorganisms, including legionella, or limit their ability to grow;

■ monitoring any control measures applied;

■ keeping records of these and other actions taken, such as maintenance and repair work.

Record keeping

24 Where there are five or more employees, the significant findings of the risk assessment must be recorded. If there are less than five employees, there is no requirement to record anything although it is useful to keep a written record.

25 Records must be retained for the period they remain current and for at least two years afterwards, with the exception of records kept for monitoring and inspection, which should be kept for at least five years. It may be helpful to keep training records of employees; records of the work of external service providers, such as water treatment specialists; and information on other hazards, eg chemical safety data sheets.

26 Records, either written or electronic, should contain accurate information about who did the work and when it was carried out. All records should be signed, verified or authenticated by a signature or other appropriate means. Records should include details of the:

■ person or people responsible for conducting the risk assessment, managing, and implementing the written scheme;

■ significant findings of the risk assessment;

■ written control scheme and details of its implementation;

■ details of the state of operation of the system, ie in use/not in use;

■ results of any monitoring, inspection, test or check carried out, the dates and any resulting corrective actions, as defined in the written scheme of precautions, such as:

 - results of chemical and microbial analysis of the water;
 - water treatment chemical usage;
 - inspections and checks on the water treatment equipment to confirm correct operation;
 - inspections and checks on the water system components and equipment to confirm correct and safe operation;
 - records of maintenance to the water system components, equipment and water treatment system;
 - the cleaning and disinfection procedures and the associated reports and certificates.

Part 1 The control of legionella bacteria in evaporative cooling systems

Legionnaires' disease: Technical guidance

Evaporative cooling systems: Types, design and operation

What is an evaporative cooling system?

1.1 Evaporative cooling of water is widely used to dissipate heat from air conditioning, refrigeration and industrial process systems.

1.2 There is a range of evaporative cooling systems that use evaporation of water to achieve the cooling effect and these include cooling towers and evaporative condensers. Open-circuit cooling towers are the most common and range in size from small packaged towers, used in air conditioning and light industrial applications, up to large towers, including hyperbolic towers, for heavy industrial, petrochemical and power generation applications. All evaporative cooling systems, except for large natural draught towers, have a fan system to force or induce airflow through the unit.

1.3 Although less common, other systems that do not rely solely on the principle of evaporation, are dry/wet coolers or condensers. These systems are able to operate in dry air-cooled mode and wet evaporative cooling mode, but when running in wet mode, may present an equivalent risk to a cooling tower or evaporative condenser and may require similar control measures.

1.4 This section gives a detailed description of the characteristics of each type of system, design and construction of evaporative cooling systems; details of their safe operation, commissioning, management and maintenance.

Safe operation and control measures

Design
1.5 A cooling system should be designed with safe operation and maintenance in mind. In particular, it should minimise the release of water droplets and be easily and safely accessible for all essential maintenance tasks. The cooling tower should be designed in a way that readily allows inspection, cleaning and disinfection of all wetted surfaces. Further information on the design of cooling systems is given in paragraph 1.22.

Commissioning and safe start-up
1.6 Systems should be commissioned by adequately trained people in a co-ordinated way to ensure that the system operates correctly as designed. The mechanical and electrical commissioning needs to be co-ordinated with disinfection and cleaning processes and the commissioning of the water treatment system to ensure that the risk of legionella growth and exposure is controlled from the start. Further information on commissioning and safe start-up is given in paragraphs 1.23–1.25

Operation and maintenance
1.7 A cooling system should be operated in a way that avoids stagnant water conditions and allows the water treatment control measures to be effective. Intermittent operation and duty/standby equipment require particular attention. The system should be maintained to ensure its correct operation and avoid loss of cooling efficiency, which may lead to an increase in microbial growth. Drift eliminators and air inlets need to be maintained to minimise the release of water droplets. There is further information on operating cooling systems in paragraphs 1.26–1.31.

Water treatment

1.8 An effective water treatment programme is an essential control measure to inhibit the growth of legionella in the cooling water. The cooling water treatment programme should be capable of controlling not only legionella and other microbial activity, but also corrosion, scale formation and fouling to maintain the system's cleanliness. Appropriate water treatment may involve a range of chemical and physical techniques to control corrosion, scaling and fouling potential of the cooling water and to control microbial growth. All of these need to be monitored regularly to ensure they remain effective.

1.9 The exact techniques that are required may vary significantly with different water supplies, cooling system design and operating conditions. Paragraphs 1.32–1.74 give further information.

Cleaning and disinfection

1.10 It is a legal duty to control the risk of exposure to legionella bacteria. As legionella are more likely to grow in a cooling system fouled with deposits, maintaining system cleanliness and the water in it is an essential part of the control regime.

1.11 The required frequency and scope of regular cleaning and disinfection operations should be determined by an assessment of the fouling potential. This should be based on inspection and the history of the water treatment control of microbial activity, scaling tendencies and other factors that may result in fouling of the particular system. In relatively clean environments with effective control measures it may be acceptable to extend the period between cleaning operations, provided you can demonstrate that system cleanliness is maintained. Paragraphs 1.77–1.113 contain detailed technical guidance on cleaning and disinfection techniques and requirements.

Water quality monitoring

1.12 The composition of the make-up and cooling water should be routinely monitored to ensure the continued effectiveness of the treatment programme. The frequency and extent will depend on the operating characteristics of the system. Paragraphs1.114–1.129 give guidance on analysis and monitoring and suggested details of monitoring schedules.

Types of evaporative cooling equipment

1.13 There is a range of evaporative cooling systems that uses evaporation of water as the means of achieving the cooling effect. These include cooling towers and evaporative condensers. Although less common, other systems that do not rely solely on the principle of evaporation are dry/wet coolers or condensers. These dry/wet systems are able to operate in dry air-cooled mode and wet evaporative cooling mode. When running in wet mode, these systems may present the equivalent risk to a cooling tower or evaporative condenser and may require similar control measures.

Cooling towers

1.14 Open-circuit cooling towers are the most common and these can have several different configurations. Figure 1.1 shows one common configuration and illustrates all the main components of an open-circuit cooling tower. Figure 1.2 demonstrates two other common configurations. Commonly, large industrial cooling towers are induced draught counterflow towers, but in air conditioning and light industrial applications, all three configurations are common.

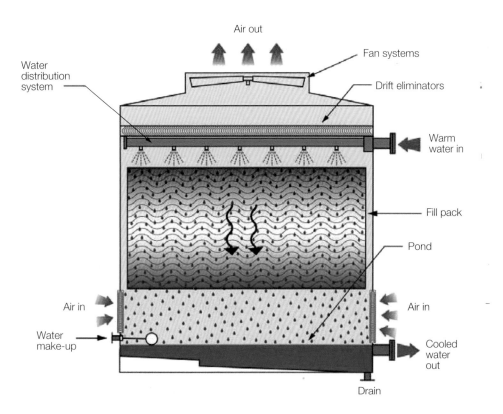

Figure 1.1 Induced draught counterflow cooling tower

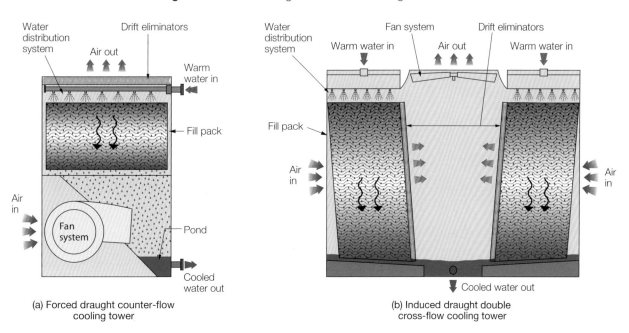

(a) Forced draught counter-flow cooling tower

(b) Induced draught double cross-flow cooling tower

Figure 1.2 Examples of a forced draught counter-flow and an induced draught double cross-flow cooling tower

1.15 In an open-circuit cooling tower, the water to be cooled is distributed over a fill pack at the same time as a fan system moves air through the fill pack. This causes a small portion of the cooling water to evaporate which reduces the temperature of the remaining circulating water. The cooled water is collected at the base of the cooling tower and then recirculated to the plant or process needing to be cooled and the warm, humid air is discharged from the tower into the atmosphere.

Evaporative condensers and closed-circuit cooling towers

1.16 Evaporative condensers use the same evaporative cooling principle as cooling towers but incorporate a heat exchanger in which a fluid is cooled by a secondary recirculating system that distributes water over the heat exchange coil and a portion of this water is evaporated (Figure 1.3a). The heat to evaporate the water is taken from the coolant, with the heat being transferred to the water vapour in the air stream, which is discharged into the atmosphere in the same way as a cooling tower. The coolant is often a refrigerant gas but where the coolant is water or a water/glycol mixture, these systems are sometimes referred to as closed-circuit cooling towers.

1.17 A closed-circuit cooling tower is designed to prevent the water to be cooled from becoming contaminated by coming into contact with the atmosphere. This can be achieved by linking to a separate heat exchanger or by a closed-circuit cooling tower (Figure 1.3b). The latter has a heat exchanger through which the water to be cooled flows and there is a secondary recirculating water system providing the cooling effect in the same way as an evaporative condenser.

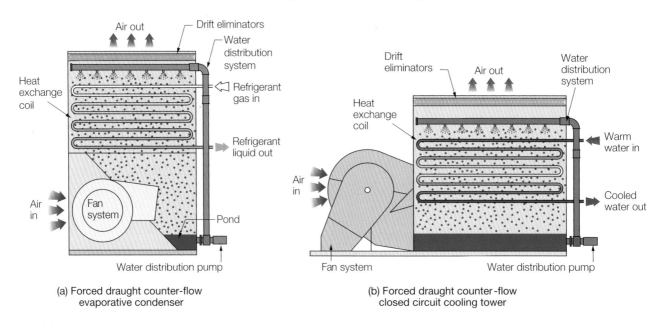

(a) Forced draught counter-flow evaporative condenser

(b) Forced draught counter-flow closed circuit cooling tower

Figure 1.3 Examples of a forced draught counter-flow evaporative condenser and a forced draught counter-flow closed circuit cooling tower

Dry/wet cooling systems

1.18 Dry/wet systems, sometimes referred to as hybrid or adiabatic coolers, are able to operate in dry air-cooled mode and wet evaporative cooling mode. They are essentially dry air coolers or condensers that use evaporative cooling to pre-cool the air when demand requires. At low ambient air temperatures or cooling load the unit runs dry without any secondary water flow. As the air temperature or load increases, the unit is switched to wet mode. When running in wet mode, these systems may present an equivalent risk as a conventional cooling tower or evaporative condenser and may require similar control measures. They only use water for evaporative cooling when the ambient air temperature or cooling load is high.

1,19 When in evaporative mode, these systems incorporate a two-stage process. The evaporation of water is used to cool the air entering the cooler, usually by spraying water into the air stream or by trickling it over a medium (eg cellulose pads or plastic mesh) through which the air passes. The cooled air then goes to a conventional dry cooler, increasing its cooling capacity. During the pre-cooling of the air, some or all of the water is evaporated.

1.20 Some of these systems may give rise to significant risk when the spray creates aerosols, or the water sprayed or trickled into the air stream is from a stored water source and/or is collected and recirculated. The risk is reduced when there is no storage or recirculation of water and where generation of aerosols is minimised. The design features of these types of systems are varied, requiring consideration of each on its merits, an assessment of the level of risk posed and the control measures required. Figure 1.4 shows three different examples of dry/ wet systems:

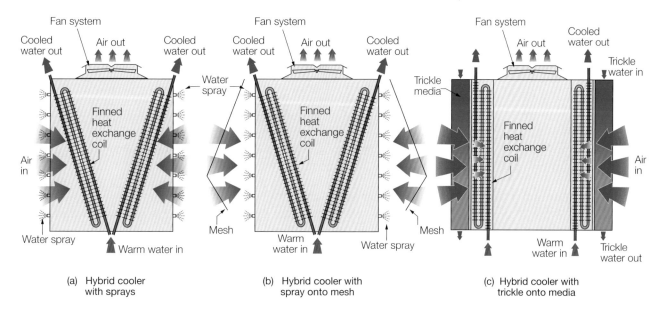

Figure 1.4 Dry/wet cooling systems

1.21 Owing to their different principles of operation, these systems may not require notification under the Notification of Cooling Towers and Evaporative Condensers Regulations 1992 (NCTEC) but it is important to assess the system against the notification requirements defined in NCTEC, eg where such systems spray water directly onto the surface of the heat exchanger.

Info box 1.1: Notification requirements under NCTEC

A 'notifiable device' means a cooling tower (a device whose main purpose is to cool water by direct contact between that water and a stream of air) or an evaporative condenser (a device whose main purpose is to cool a fluid by passing that fluid through a heat exchanger which is itself cooled by contact with water passing through a stream of air) except where it contains no water that is exposed to air; where its water supply is not connected; and where its electrical supply is not connected.

Design and construction

1.22 Evaporative cooling systems should be designed and constructed to facilitate safe operation and maintenance, help cleaning and disinfection and control the release of water droplets. In particular, consider the following:

- Cooling towers and evaporative condensers should be made of corrosion-resistant materials that are easy to clean and disinfect. Smaller units are typically constructed from mild steel (with a protective coating), stainless steel or glass reinforced plastic (GRP). Large industrial towers are normally concrete or treated timber construction. Fill packs and drift eliminators are usually made of PVC or polypropylene. The heat exchange coils in evaporative condensers and closed-circuit cooling towers are galvanised steel, stainless steel or copper construction. Construction components made from materials such as natural rubber and untreated timber, which support microbial growth, should be avoided.

- Cooling towers and evaporative condensers require large amounts of fresh ambient air that acts as the medium to remove the heat and which is then discharged into the atmosphere containing water vapour. Towers should therefore be located so that there is an unimpeded supply of ambient air and no obstruction to the exhaust stream from the tower. Ideally, towers should not be located near to any air conditioning or ventilation inlets not close to open windows. There should be adequate space around the tower for routine maintenance and inspection; and gantries or platforms, access doors and hatches, so that all parts of the equipment that require inspection and maintenance can be safely accessed.

- Drift eliminators should be installed in all towers that have fans. Some large natural draught towers have very slow exhaust speeds and the drift loss is negligible. In spite of the name, the function of a drift eliminator is to 'reduce' rather than actually 'eliminate' aerosol drift, although some types are more effective than others. Modern drift eliminators should reduce the drift loss to less than 0.01% of the water flow through the tower.

- In most cases, drift eliminators should be in sections that are easy to handle and readily removable for cleaning. They should be well fitted with no obvious gaps between sections and not damaged. It is important that the airflow is not impeded, eg by build-up of scale. Drift eliminators can become brittle due to chemical attack, ultraviolet radiation from the sun or temperature extremes. Brittleness will lead to breakage of the plastic and this will affect the efficiency of the eliminator. The efficacy of drift elimination is dependent on the relationship between fan speeds, density and resistance of the pack, as well as the design and fitting of the eliminator itself. Care should be taken to ensure that effective drift elimination is maintained and the effects of any alterations to key components of the tower assessed.

- The base tank or pond of cooling towers should be fully enclosed to prevent direct sunlight onto the water. The bottom of the tank or pond should be sloped, or otherwise designed, to facilitate draining with a suitably sized drain connection at the lowest point.

- The air inlets should be designed and protected so as to minimise splash-out or windage losses and to avoid leaves and other contaminating debris being drawn into the tower.

- The water pipework, including balance pipes, should be as simple as practicable, avoiding deadlegs and sections that cannot be drained, which can lead to stagnation, allowing microbial growth. If standby pumps are fitted, any stagnant sections should be flushed with biocide-treated water periodically, typically once every week. If not managed effectively, subsequent disturbance of a deadleg may result in rapid colonisation of the whole system. The pipework should be constructed from materials compatible with the evaporative cooling equipment to reduce the possibility of corrosion.

- Cleanliness of the tower and associated plant is vital for the safe operation of a cooling system and effective cleaning should be carried out periodically. All wetted parts such as the internal surfaces of the tower, drift eliminators, water distribution system and fill pack should be accessible for an assessment of cleanliness and cleaned as needed.

- The tower should be made of materials that do not support microbial growth and can be readily disinfected. Treated timber may still be used in the manufacture of the cooling towers but it needs to be resistant to decay and easy to clean and disinfect.

■ Control of the operating water level in a cooling tower is important to prevent overflow or splash-out, which can affect treatment chemical levels and also result in the release of aerosols. Water level is often controlled by a mechanical float-operated valve, which works well for continuously operated towers. Electrical water-level devices are recommended for more precise level control and for towers that are shut down more frequently than once every quarter.

■ Tower fans are commonly automatically controlled by frequency inverters which ensure that the fan speed responds to the system load. Frequency inverters also regulate the air speed through the drift eliminators, which in turn will limit the amount of drift exiting from the tower.

Commissioning

1.23 Commissioning of cooling systems is an essential step in ensuring they operate safely from the outset. Cases of legionellosis have been associated with systems that were not clean or properly commissioned before being put into operation.

1.24 Systems should be commissioned to ensure they operate correctly and safely in accordance with the design parameters. It is essential that the commissioning process is carried out in a logical and defined manner in full compliance with the supplier's or installer's instructions and includes both the evaporative cooling equipment itself as well as any associated pipework and water treatment plant. The responsibilities of the staff carrying out the commissioning process should be clearly defined with adequate time and resources allocated to allow the integrated parts of the installation to be commissioned correctly. The precautions taken to prevent or control the risk of exposure to legionella during normal operation of cooling systems also apply to the commissioning process.

1.25 When scheduling commissioning (or recommissioning) of a tower, note the following:

■ Commissioning should not be carried out until the system is required for use and it should not be charged with water until commissioning takes place. If filled for hydraulic testing, the system should be drained and not refilled until commissioning takes place.

■ If a new system is to be taken into use within a week, commissioning can be carried out and the system left charged with treated water, which should include a biocide.

■ Record the results of the commissioning process and include them as a section in the operation and maintenance manual. The availability of such baseline data enables periodic checks to be made to show that the installation continues to operate as intended.

■ Formal arrangements should be made to check that commissioning has been completed to the standard specified, eg an independent engineer witnesses the testing and countersigns the relevant documents.

Management of cooling systems

1.26 A cooling system consists of a cooling tower, evaporative condenser or other cooling equipment, together with pumps, recirculation pipework and valves and usually the heat exchanger or condenser. It may also include ancillary items, such as make-up supply tanks, pre-treatment plant and the chemical dosing system. All these items need to be considered and included in the management and control scheme of the system, including:

- correct operation and maintenance – this is the basic requirement for ensuring the safety of the system;
- cleanliness – keeping the system clean reduces the possibility of it harbouring bacteria and their uncontrolled growth and will allow effective application of elements of the water treatment regime, such as biocide dosing;
- suitable water treatment – this minimises the opportunity for bacteria to proliferate within the system as well as controlling scaling, corrosion and fouling;
- effective drift eliminators – these act as the last line of defence, minimising the loss of potentially infectious aerosols if there is a failure of the water treatment regime.

Operation

1.27 The cooling system should be kept in regular use whenever possible. When a system is used intermittently, arrangements should be in place to ensure that treated water circulates through the entire system, this should be monitored and records kept. The system, including the fans, should run for long enough to distribute the treated water thoroughly.

1.28 If a system is to be out of use for a week or longer, eg up to a month, biocides should continue to be dosed and circulated throughout the system, at least weekly. If a system is to be out of use for longer than a month it should be drained and shut down. The system, including the water treatment regime, should be recommissioned before reuse.

1.29 An operation and maintenance manual should be available for the whole system and include the manufacturers' instructions for all individual pieces of equipment, and details of:

- operation and maintenance procedures that enable plant operators to carry out their duties safely and effectively;
- checks equipment as fitted;
- the system as currently in operation;
- schematic diagram and total water volume of the system;
- specific information on the water treatment programme;
- normal operation control parameters and limits;
- required corrective actions for out-of-specification situations, such as when plant operating conditions or the make-up water quality change;
- cleaning and disinfection procedures;
- monitoring records of the system operation.

Maintenance

1.30 Preventive maintenance is an important measure to assure reliable and safe operation of the cooling system. The operation and maintenance manual should include a detailed maintenance schedule, listing the various time intervals when the system plant and water should be checked, inspected, overhauled or cleaned. The completion of every task should be recorded by the plant operatives.

1.31 Drift eliminators require particular attention with regard to maintenance. To remain effective, they should be regularly inspected to ensure they are clean, properly positioned and not damaged.

Requirements of a cooling water treatment programme

1.32 An effective water treatment programme should be established based on the physical and operating parameters for the cooling system and a thorough analysis of the make-up water. The components of the water treatment programme should be environmentally acceptable and comply with any local discharge requirements.

1.33 This section covers the key principles involved in the development of a suitable cooling water treatment programme for the control of legionella and offers guidance on how to treat water in cooling systems.

Desired outcomes

1.34 An appropriate cooling water treatment programme must be capable of controlling not only legionella and other microbial activity, but also corrosion, scale formation and fouling, and include appropriate measures, such as regular physical cleaning and disinfection, to maintain the system's cleanliness. This is very important since these aspects are often interrelated and failure to control one aspect will often lead to other problems and will increase the legionella risk.

1.35 The water treatment programme should be capable of delivering certain desired outcomes. Table 1.1 shows the typical cooling water desired outcomes. These outcomes will depend on the nature of the water and the system being treated. The particular desired outcomes and the metrics to be used should be agreed between the system owner/operator and their specialist water treatment service provider.

Table 1.1 Typical cooling water desired outcomes

Aspect of control	Desired outcome
Microbial activity, as estimated by dip slides or TVCs (total viable counts, at 30 °C (minimum 48 hrs incubation)	Not greater than 1×10^4 cfu/ml (colony forming units per millilitre)
Legionella	Not detected or not greater than 100 cfu/l
Corrosion of carbon steel	Generally less than 5 mpy and preferably less than 2 mpy
Scale control	No significant loss of hardness from solution (eg a calcium balance of >0.9) Minimal visible deposition of hardness salts on pack or other surfaces and no significant loss of heat transfer efficiency as a result of deposition
Physical fouling and system cleanliness	Bulk water should be visually clear and the frequency of physical cleaning and disinfection should reflect the tendency of the system to build up fouling deposits as a result of airborne or process contamination or microbial growth

---

Info box 1.2: Scientific (or standard) notation

Scientific notation is a compact way of expressing either very large or very small numbers and makes the number easier to work with. The format for a number in scientific notation is the product of a number (integer or decimal) and a power of 10 and is simple to express, as shown in the examples used in this guidance: 10^4 = 10 000, 10^3 = 1000.

Microbial control

1.36 The operating conditions of a cooling system provide an environment where microorganisms can proliferate. The water temperatures, pH conditions, concentration of nutrients, presence of dissolved oxygen, carbon dioxide and daylight, together with large surface areas, all favour the growth of microorganisms such as protozoa, algae, fungi and bacteria, including legionella.

1.37 Problems arise when microorganisms are allowed to grow to excess. This can result in the formation of biofilms on system surfaces. These can:

- cause a reduction in heat transfer;
- harbour and protect legionella and provide an environment for their growth;
- induce highly localised microbial corrosion;
- interfere with the effectiveness of corrosion inhibitors;
- trap particulate matter, increasing the problem of fouling;
- disrupt water distribution within the tower.

1.38 Both surface-adhering (sessile) and free-flowing (planktonic) bacteria need to be controlled for a complete and effective programme. Microbial activity is generally controlled by using biocides, which are chemical additives that kill microorganisms. Whatever biocide regime or other microbial control measure is used, it should be capable of maintaining consistently low aerobic counts, often referred to as total viable counts (TVCs) and prevent the proliferation of legionella.

Corrosion control

1.39 In many cooling systems, a significant proportion of the construction material is mild steel, which is susceptible to corrosion. Although heat transfer equipment may be made of more corrosion-resistant metals such as copper, copper alloys or stainless steel, these metals also need to be adequately protected. Corrosion of mild steel, in particular, should be inhibited as it may lead to conditions that encourage the growth of legionella.

1.40 Good corrosion control requires a clear understanding of the cooling water chemistry and metallurgy, the selection of a corrosion inhibitor matched to that chemistry and metallurgy and adequate control of both the inhibitor and the chemistry within the system. As with all cooling water analysis a suitably trained and competent person should interpret the results.

> ## Info box 1.3: Corrosion rates
>
> Corrosion rates are commonly expressed in mpy (mils per year) where a mil is 1/1000th of an inch penetration. The metric units for corrosion rates are mm/a (millimetres per annum), and as an example, a corrosion rate of 1.0 mpy is the same as 0.0254 mm/a. These general values are for 'typical' cooling systems with 'typical' waters. For certain process cooling applications different corrosion level targets (either higher or lower) may be appropriate. Corrosion control will normally be achieved either by adding specific corrosion inhibitors or by allowing the cooling water to concentrate to a point where it becomes less corrosive but more scale-forming in nature, and treated with appropriate scale inhibitors and dispersants.
>
> Corrosion rates can be determined using metal corrosion coupons or electronic instrumentation. Such analysis is not typically included in a water treatment programme for smaller cooling systems unless it is a contractual requirement, but it is considered good practice. The measurement of total iron levels in the recirculating water can give some indication of corrosion activity, but because iron readily oxidises in an oxygenated environment to form insoluble deposits, the result is open to misinterpretation. A typical control limit for total iron would be less than 1.0 mg/l and while a higher level may well be an indication of inadequate corrosion control, a level of less than 1.0 mg/l does not definitively indicate good corrosion control.

1.41 Corrosion and scale inhibitors should be applied continuously and be capable of producing the desired control over corrosion and scaling. For liquid inhibitors a commonly employed method of addition is using a dosing pump controlled by a water meter installed on the cooling system make-up water supply. In situ monitoring of treatment reserves, with feedback control of dosing, can also be employed.

1.42 Inhibitor formulations can be supplied as a single multi-functional product incorporating a number of corrosion and scale inhibitors, and dispersant polymers to reduce fouling tendencies. For some large cooling systems, it can be more cost effective, and provide greater flexibility if the required components are supplied and dosed separately.

Scale control

1.43 Scale is the localised precipitation of normally water-soluble inorganic hardness salts. Its formation is influenced by the concentration of calcium salts, pH, surface and bulk water temperatures and the concentration of the total dissolved solids. As an evaporative cooling system operates, the concentration of these various dissolved solids increases and the pH of the water tends to rise, which results in the scaling potential of the water increasing.

1.44 Scale formation results in loss of heat transfer, reduced flow rates and loss of efficiency, and contributes to deposition. Legionella can be associated with such deposits. The scale protects the bacteria and so reduces the effectiveness of any biocidal treatment.

1.45 One or more of the following techniques generally control scale formation:

■ removing the hardness from the make-up water by pre-treatment, eg water softening;

- adding specific scale inhibitors that extend the solubility of the hardness salts and so prevent precipitation;
- acid dosing to lower the pH and alkalinity and reduce the scaling potential;
- limiting the system concentration factor to a range within which the hardness salts can remain soluble.

Info box 1.4: Scaling index

The scaling tendency of a given water can be predicted by calculating the Langelier Saturation Index or Ryznar Stability Index. Assessing control of scaling can be made using tools such as calcium balance, which estimates how much of the calcium hardness entering the cooling system is being maintained in solution. As with all cooling water analysis, a suitably trained and competent person should interpret the results.

Fouling control and physical cleanliness

1.46 'Fouling' is normally applied to deposition of particulate material and debris such as:

- insoluble corrosion products;
- scale deposits;
- mud, silt, clay;
- airborne dust and debris;
- process contaminants;
- biological matter such as insects, pollen and plant material, and the formation of biofilm.

1.47 Settlement will occur in low-velocity areas of the system and can lead to loss of plant performance, corrosion under the deposits, increased microbial activity and proliferation of legionella. In systems using make-up water that has a high concentration of suspended solids, pre-clarification may be needed.

1.48 Fouling tendencies can be controlled by adding specific dispersant chemicals to keep suspended solids mobile and may be helped by incorporating side-stream filtration which filters a proportion of the circulating water and then returns it to the cooling circuit. The frequency of disinfection and cleaning operations should be determined by the tendency for parts of the system such as sumps and the pack to become fouled with accumulated deposits. An evaporative cooling system is, in effect, an air scrubber, so some build-up of deposits with time is inevitable and periodic removal of these deposits is an important measure in the control of legionella.

1.49 Effective water treatment can significantly reduce the fouling in a cooling system and the history of control of the fouling factors and water treatment programme should be used in conjunction with inspection to determine the frequency and type of cleaning and disinfection operations to be carried out.

1.50 Off-line disinfection and cleaning is not an end in itself. The desired outcome is system cleanliness, and if this can be achieved effectively by other means on an ongoing basis, this is acceptable.

Conventional chemical water treatment

1.51 Most cooling systems are treated using what might be termed conventional chemical techniques. This may involve adding inhibitors to control corrosion and scale formation, biocides to control microbial growth and dispersants to control fouling. These may be in the form of single-function chemicals or multi-functional admixtures.

1.52 The chemical programme can be augmented by pre-treatment of the make-up water and will include bleed-off control to limit the cycles of concentration. In some instances, acid dosing may be incorporated as part of the scale control programme and in other instances side-stream filtration may be employed to control the build-up of suspended solids.

1.53 This chemical treatment programme should be carefully selected based on the cooling system design, size (ie the water chemistry in smaller volume systems may be more difficult to maintain) and operating conditions, the make-up water analysis, materials of the system construction and environmental constraints. The different elements of the treatment programme should be chemically compatible.

1.54 The treatment programme should be capable of coping with variations in the operating conditions, make-up water analysis and microbial loading.

1.55 Chemical dosage and control should be automated where possible to ensure the correct treatment levels are consistently applied and to minimise exposure of operators to chemical hazards. For each chemical. there should be a safety data sheet, a completed COSHH risk assessment and control measures applied for their safe handling and use.

Biocides

1.56 The biocide regime should be capable of controlling the microbial activity in the cooling water consistently, so the total viable count (TVC) of aerobic bacteria is maintained at no greater than 1×10^4 cfu/ml (colony forming units per millilitre) and other problematic microbes are controlled. The ease with which this can be achieved will vary from system to system depending on the operating conditions and particularly the availability of nutrient in the water to support microbial growth.

1.57 The dosage and control of the biocide regime should be automated to ensure the correct quantity of biocide is applied at the required frequency. The dosage of oxidising biocides, such as bromine and chlorine, can be controlled by a redox or amperometric control system, which automatically adjusts the dosage in response to the oxidant demand of the water to maintain the desired biocide residual level.

1.58 An advantage of oxidising biocides is that they can be monitored by a simple field test to measure the residual biocide in the cooling water, whereas the concentration of non-oxidising biocides cannot easily be measured directly.

1.59 Biocides are applied routinely at the tower pond or the suction side of the recirculating water pump, but should be dosed so that the biocide will circulate throughout the cooling system. However, in air conditioning systems where the tower can be bypassed, the biocide needs to be added to the suction side of the recirculating pump. Whatever method is used, it should ensure good mixing and avoid localised high concentration of chemical, which may cause corrosion.

1.60 The effectiveness of the biocide regime should be monitored weekly, conventionally by using appropriate microbial dip slides (although alternative technologies that do not rely on culturing bacteria also allow analysis of microbial activity), and specific sampling for legionella should be done on at least a quarterly basis. Adjustments to the dosage and control settings may be needed in response to any high count. More frequent sampling may be needed for other reasons (see paragraph 1.126).

Info box 1.5: Biocide types and application

Oxidising biocides

The oxidising biocides most commonly used in cooling water are those based on compounds of the halogens chlorine and bromine and may be supplied as solid tablets, granules or powder, or as solutions. On dilution these compounds form the free halogen species hypochlorous acid (HOCl), hypobromous acid (HOBr), hypochorite ion (OCl⁻) and hypobromite ion (OBr⁻) in a pH-dependent equilibrium.

This pH-dependent relationship is important because the hypochlorous and hypobromous acids are more active biocidally than the hypochlorite and hypobromite ions and the concentration of these active acids decline with rising pH. As the pH of cooling water rises and becomes increasingly alkaline, chlorine compounds tend to become less biocidally active and slower acting, whereas bromine compounds retain much of their activity. For this reason the use of chlorine-based biocide programmes tend to be restricted to larger cooling systems operating at lower cycles of concentration or those employing pH control. Bromine-based biocide programmes are generally considered more appropriate for smaller cooling systems and any system where the cooling water pH is likely to exceed pH 8.

A chlorine-based programme can effectively be converted to a bromine-based programme by adding an inorganic bromide salt, which converts the hypochlorous species to the hypobromous equivalent with a requisite increase in biocidal activity at higher pHs.

Halogen-based biocides are typically applied to establish a measurable reserve using DPD No1, in the range 0.5–1.0 mg/l as Cl_2 or 1.0–2.0 mg/l as Br_2. In some circumstances, it may be possible to maintain good microbial control at a lower halogen reserve and in other circumstances, such as more alkaline pH conditions, it may be necessary to increase the halogen reserve to compensate for the reduction in biocidal activity. You should monitor the effectiveness of the microbial control using weekly dip slides and periodic legionella analysis (see the control values in Tables 1.8 and 1.9) and adjust the target biocide reserves accordingly.

It is preferable that oxidising biocides are applied continuously or in response to a redox or amperometric control system, pre-set at a level equivalent to the correct halogen reserve required. If, however, halogen biocides are shot dosed, they should be dosed sufficiently often and in sufficient quantity to maintain good microbial control at all times (see the control values in Tables 1.8 and 1.9).

Oxidising biocides are aggressive chemicals and if overdosed will lead to increased corrosion rates. High concentrations of oxidising biocides can also degrade other cooling water chemicals, such as inhibitors, so it is important that the dosing arrangements are designed to ensure the two chemicals do not mix until they are well diluted, ie in the system.

Owing to their mode of action, oxidising biocides are not prone to developing microbial resistance, so it is not normally necessary to dose a second biocide alternately, unless the oxidising biocide is dosed infrequently. However, bio-dispersant chemicals, which are special surfactants, are often applied in conjunction with oxidising biocides to help the penetration and dispersion of biofilms. While it is not normally necessary to dose a secondary biocide where an oxidising biocide is applied continuously, it may be appropriate to control a particular microbial problem such as algal growth in areas of the cooling tower exposed to sunlight.

Used correctly, both chlorine and bromine biocide programmes are extremely effective at controlling the general microbial count and preventing the proliferation of legionella even where significant nutrient levels are present. Their efficacy can, however, be affected by certain process contaminants such as ammonia or very high organic loading. Under such circumstances an alternative oxidising biocide such as chlorine dioxide or an appropriate non-oxidising biocide programme may be used.

The performance of chlorine dioxide as a biocide is not affected by the water pH, it does not react with ammoniacal compounds and it is often less affected by organic contamination than either chlorine- or bromine-based oxidising biocides. It is extremely effective at penetrating and dispersing biofilms. However, it is more complex to dose and its volatility means that maintaining a measurable residual of chlorine dioxide in the recirculating water downstream of the cooling tower may prove difficult. It tends therefore to be used as a niche biocide for applications where contamination precludes the use of chlorine or bromine. When it is used, it may either be dosed continuously at a low level or intermittently at a higher level with the frequency and dosage level often being determined by the results of microbial monitoring rather than by achieving and maintaining a specific chlorine dioxide residual.

Non-oxidising biocides

Non-oxidising biocides are organic compounds that are usually more complex than oxidising biocides. They are generally more stable and persistent in the cooling water than oxidising biocides, but their concentration will reduce with time because of system water losses and degradation and consumption of the active material.

To achieve the right non-oxidising biocide concentration to kill microorganisms, biocide is normally added as a shot dose. The frequency and volume of applications are dependent on system volume, system half-life, re-infection rate and the required biocide contact time, typically at least four hours. These need to be considered to ensure that the biocide concentration necessary to kill the microorganisms is achieved. In systems with smaller water volumes and high evaporation rates it is particularly important that the above parameters are accurately determined. In the case of systems that have long retention times, the half-life of the biocide is the controlling factor. The total system volume should be established to ensure that the desired levels of non-oxidising biocides are applied.

A non-oxidising biocide programme should use two biocides with different kill mechanisms on an alternating basis to minimise the risk of the microbial flora evolving into a population tolerant to a single biocide type. Once the concentration of any biocide has been depleted to below its effective level, the system will be open to infection. The efficacy of non-oxidising biocides may be influenced by the pH and temperature of the water in the system and this should be taken into account to ensure that the biocide programme is effective. The following points are important in selecting a non-oxidising biocide programme:

- retention time and system half-life;
- cooling water analysis, eg pH;
- microbial populations;
- system dynamics;
- system contaminants;
- handling precautions;
- effluent constraints;
- considering if an oxidising biocide programme is more appropriate.

Pre-treatment

1.61 Make-up water is normally mains water but can be supplied from various sources, such as rivers, lakes and boreholes, or even from within the process itself. These sources may require pre-treatment to reduce contamination and improve the quality to that approaching mains supply. If not pre-treated to mains quality then the water entering the system will often be subject to considerable variations in suspended solids, total dissolved solids and microbial composition. This should be considered in the risk assessment for the cooling system and a strategy will be required to manage it.

1.62 Pre-treatment may take the form of filtration or clarification to remove suspended solids, disinfection to reduce the microbial population, reverse osmosis to reduce the dissolved solids or softening to reduce the hardness level and scaling potential.

1.63 Water softening is often used as a pre-treatment in hard water areas and can prevent scale formation effectively. However, removing all the hardness significantly increases the corrosivity of cooling water. This can be extremely damaging to the cooling equipment and may invalidate the manufacturer's warranty. It is common therefore to blend a proportion of hard water back into a softened make-up water supply. Reverse osmosis permeate is also occasionally used to provide softened make-up water to cooling systems. Without blending back of some hardness and alkalinity salts, this water is even more corrosive than softened water.

Intermittently operated systems and standby equipment

1.64 Cooling systems that remain idle for more than a few days or that are held on wet standby for use at short notice should be dosed with an appropriate biocide and circulated to ensure thorough mixing at least once a week.

1.65 Where a system has duty and standby equipment such as circulation pumps, these should all be operated during the circulation period to ensure that the biocide reaches all parts of the system and to avoid stagnation.

1.66 Where part of a system, eg a chiller plant, is brought back into service after a period of being on standby, the whole system should be dosed with biocide. It may be desirable to maintain higher levels of chemical treatments, particularly corrosion inhibitors, at such times.

Alternative treatment techniques

1.67 There are a number of alternative techniques of water treatment available and these methods of control are sometimes used singularly as a stand-alone technology or in combination with traditional chemical biocides. As with the application of water treatment chemicals, owners/operators of cooling systems will need to monitor the efficacy of such control processes since the appropriateness and effectiveness of these techniques can vary significantly. The owner/operator of the cooling system should verify that the proposed technique is suitable for the particular application, taking into account the specific make-up water characteristics, operating conditions and desired outcomes. The alternative techniques of water treatment available include the following.

Ultraviolet irradiation (usually used in conjunction with a biocide)

1.68 UV irradiation has been used to treat water systems for many years, particularly where the water is 'highly polished', ie good quality with little suspended solids and hardness. This physical control process uses the UV part of the electromagnetic spectrum (between visible light and X-rays) to cause damage to the microorganism's cellular genetic material (DNA). At a wavelength of 265 nm, UV is found to be most effective. Typically used in conjunction with a filtration device upstream of the UV lamp in domestic water services, in cooling systems UV is more frequently used in conjunction with a chemical biocide. The quality of the cooling water is an important consideration, as hardness and iron can lead to scaling or staining of lamp surfaces.

Use of ozone

1.69 Ozone can be used as a fast-acting, rapidly dissipating biocide which exhibits broad spectrum antimicrobial activity. Within cooling system applications, the potential for a short half-life due to rapid decomposition may result in areas of the system remaining untreated. This will be prevalent especially in the remote parts of a large cooling system with a long holding time. Also consider the reactivity of ozone with other system treatment products (eg scale and corrosion inhibitors).

Electromagnetic/pulsed electric field technologies

1.70 This technology is based on pulses of electromagnetic energy inactivating/ disrupting the cellular structures within microorganisms. The production of 'free radicals' on exposure to electromagnetic pulses is also thought to contribute to antimicrobial action by electrochemical reaction.

Ultrasonics and cavitation

1.71 The interaction of ultrasonic energy with water results in cavitation processes, generating cavitation bubbles, which when they collapse can lead to inactivation of microorganisms. This process is called sonication. This process is short lived and so the treatment programme used often incorporates a chemical application too.

Filtration technologies

1.72 By nature of their action, cooling systems may suffer considerable levels of system contamination, either by suspended solids in the make-up water, or the 'scrubbing action' of cooling towers, or by process leaks encouraging microbial activity. Side-stream filtration, where a volume of recirculating cooling water is passed through a 'side-stream' loop, is commonly employed in large cooling systems where the plant operates continuously, but the principle may be employed in most cooling systems, usually depending on economic justification.

Establishing performance criteria for microbiological control programmes

1.73 Whatever means is used for microbial control, it should be monitored rigorously to ensure control is maintained. Where possible, performance criteria for other non-chemical techniques should be established and monitored.

1.74 When introducing an alternative treatment technique, more frequent microbial monitoring should be considered until control is established.

Inspection, cleaning and disinfection procedures

1.75 Maintaining the cleanliness of the cooling system and the water in it is critical to prevent or control the risk of exposure to legionella. This section gives guidance on when and how to inspect, clean and disinfect a cooling system.

1.76 Decisions about the frequency and scope of inspection and cleaning operations and whether a cooling system is clean enough for operation are ultimately the responsibility of the responsible person(s). They may seek advice and help from specialist service providers for water treatment, risk assessment, cleaning and disinfection.

Why is it important to clean and disinfect the cooling system?

1.77 Legionella are more likely to proliferate in water systems that are fouled with deposits and biofilm that can protect the organisms from water treatments and provide nutrients for them to multiply. So maintaining system cleanliness is crucial.

1.78 Effective water treatment measures can reduce the rate at which a cooling system becomes fouled, however, an evaporative cooling system will inevitably accumulate airborne dust from the atmosphere and may be subject to contamination originating from the process for which the system provides cooling. It is therefore necessary to take cooling systems out of service periodically for physical, and possibly chemical, cleaning to remove this fouling.

When and how often should a cooling system be cleaned and disinfected?

1.79 If a system can be shown to be free from fouling, ie the deposition of particulate material and debris, there is no need for it to be cleaned at a set time interval, rather the system should be cleaned whenever it is known or suspected to have become fouled. However, as cleaning operations are disruptive, it is common to adopt a precautionary approach, with cleaning operations being scheduled to coincide with planned shutdowns or at a predetermined interval, eg six monthly.

1.80 A cooling system should always be inspected, disinfected and, if required, cleaned if there is a significant change in operation status such as:

- immediately before the system is first commissioned;
- after any prolonged shutdown of a month or longer (a risk assessment may indicate the need for cleaning and disinfection after a period of less than one month, especially in summer and for health care premises where shutdown is for more than five days);
- if the tower or any part of the cooling system has been physically altered, eg refurbishment or replacement of pumps, pipework or heat exchangers.

1.81 The tendency of the system to become fouled either with waterborne foulants or airborne contaminants will inform how often cleaning takes place. Systems should be cleaned whenever an inspection indicates the need or in response to circumstances resulting in contamination or increased fouling, such as process contamination, local construction work or an increase in the turbidity of the make-up water source.

1.82 Where a cooling system operates continuously, and it is therefore only possible for the system to be completely shut down infrequently, additional control measures and monitoring may be required to ensure cleanliness and minimise the risk. Such measures may include:

- continuous automated dosage and control of oxidising biocide;
- maintaining the correct pH level when using oxidising biocides;
- dosage of additional dispersants and biodispersants;
- side-stream filtration, possibly linked to a cooling tower basin sweeping system;
- more frequent microbial monitoring (eg monthly legionella sampling);
- online disinfection procedures;
- partial system shut-downs (eg single cooling tower cells) to allow inspection and cleaning of that part of the system.

When and how often should a cooling system be inspected?

1.83 Effective water treatment will slow the rate of fouling but will not completely eliminate it or prevent fouling caused by airborne contamination. It is therefore necessary to inspect parts of the cooling tower system regularly to determine the cleanliness, need for cleaning and type of cleaning process required. Provision should be made to allow access to these parts safely.

1.84 The frequency with which these inspections should be scheduled will vary depending on the fouling potential and should be determined by the history of previous cleans and an assessment of the likelihood of fouling, based on the water treatment history and the environment in which the cooling tower is operating. The following timescales, though not prescriptive, can be considered typical for different situations:

- at least every 3 months for a cooling system in a dirty environment (eg a tower that is prone to process or environmental contamination);
- at least twice a year for an air conditioning comfort cooling system;
- at least every 12 months for a 'clean' industrial application and any others.

1.85 Paragraphs 1.114–1.129 provide guidance on the tests for monitoring water quality and water treatment analytical reports. The responsible person(s) and their water treatment provider should review the results jointly and agree any necessary actions. In addition to the monthly water treatment reports, Table 1.2 illustrates how the history of the water analysis and other fouling factors might help decide how often to inspect and clean the system and predict the risk of an increase in fouling over a period.

Table 1.2 Example of how to use water analysis results and other fouling factors to predict risk of fouling

	Indicator (where applicable)	Good	Probably acceptable	Caution	High risk	Notes on interpretation
Microbial control indicators	Average dip slide/ TVC values	10^3 cfu/ml	10^4 cfu/ml	10^5 cfu/ml	10^6 cfu/ml	The higher the TVC, the greater the risk of biofilm formation/biofouling. An occasional high value is generally not a major concern provided the normal value is low
	Average bromine or chlorine (ppm)	>1.0 Br_2 or >0.5 Cl_2	0.5–1.0 Br_2 or 0.25–0.5 Cl_2	0.25–0.5 Br_2 or 0.1–0.25 Cl_2	0	With oxidising biocides like bromine or chlorine, maintaining a consistently good reserve minimises the risk of biofouling and controls potential legionella growth. Different values may apply for other oxidising biocides and the general principle of good control minimising fouling and legionella growth potential applies to any biocide regime. If the dip slide readings are high, the biocide regime is not effective
	Legionella +ve (per 4 samples)	0/4	0/4	¼	2/4	The absence of legionella does not indicate the absence of risk. Sporadic legionella positive results are not uncommon (even with low TVCs) and, provided the TVCs and biocide control are good, is not normally a major cause for concern. However, repeated legionella positives or positives plus poor biocide control and/or poor TVCs are and should be investigated
Scaling risk indicators	Average LSI (actual and theoretical calculation based on cycled make-up water)	1	1.5	2	2.5	As the LSI increases the risk of scale formation increases, however, a good scale inhibitor is capable of preventing scale formation up to an LSI of +2.5 and possibly beyond. Equally, with poor inhibition scale formation is likely at lower LSIs. Ideally, a comparison should be made between the actual measured LSI and the calculated theoretical LSI based on cycled up make-up water to ensure that they are similar. If the actual value is substantially lower than the theoretical value, it indicates loss of hardness from solution and so scale formation may be occurring. This indicator should be used in conjunction with the calcium balance, knowledge of the performance capabilities and history of control of the inhibitor to decide the likelihood of fouling with scale. This indicator is not valid for fully softened make-up water but a history of efficient softener operation will be adequate to ensure a low risk of scale formation
	Average calcium balance	>0.95	0.9	0.8	<0.75	The calcium balance only applies for unsoftened water and is an indicator of whether the hardness is being retained in solution or is possibly depositing on heat transfer surfaces or the packing. The lower the calcium balance, the more likelihood that scale formation is occurring
	Average level inhibitor as % of target	100% +	90%	80%	<50%	Poor control over the inhibitor significantly increases risk of scale formation and corrosion

Table 1.2 Example of how to use water analysis results and other fouling factors to predict risk of fouling (continued)

Other foulant risk indicators	Silt/suspended solids level in incoming water	Absent	Light	Moderate	Significant	High levels of silt or suspended solids in the incoming water supply can cause heavy fouling. This risk can be generally considered absent with mains water, but may be very significant with some surface water and industrial water supplies
	Process contamination	Absent	Light	Moderate	Significant	The fouling potential will depend on the nature of the contamination. Some contaminants may foul in their own right, whereas others may be a nutrient source for microbial activity, which if not adequately controlled could lead to significant biofouling. This risk factor is likely to be absent in comfort cooling and many light industrial applications
	Potential for atmospheric dust contamination	Minimal	Light	Moderate	Significant	All cooling systems will scrub contaminants from the atmosphere. The likelihood of these leading to fouling will depend on the amount of dust. The potential for this to result in fouling may also be influenced by the biofouling potential which if high may provide the 'glue' which binds the dust together to form an adherent deposit. The risk of this type of fouling is probably minimal for a comfort cooling or light industrial application with good microbial control, but may be increased significantly by local building work or a nearby industrial process, which raises the atmospheric dust level

This matrix is an example of how the system operator and their specialist water treatment service provider can use the operational history to help predict the likelihood of an increase in the level of fouling in the cooling system since the last inspection/cleaning operation. Looking at a range of factors that influence whether the system is likely to have become more fouled may help determine the need for inspection and approach required to cleaning at the next shutdown. The indicators chosen are just that, requiring interpretation, and would need to be adapted to specific situations. If all the indicators are 'good' then it is highly likely that system condition will not have deteriorated significantly since the last inspection (other than the normal build-up of sediment in sumps). If that inspection concluded that the system condition was satisfactory, it may only be necessary to verify that is still the case by limited inspection. If, on the other hand, a number of indicators score a 'high risk', increased fouling is highly likely and the planned inspection and cleaning regime will need to reflect this. Where possible, a thorough baseline inspection should be carried out to establish and record the system and pack condition at the start. Where that is not possible, a matrix like this may be used to assess retrospectively the likelihood of fouling, based on prior history.

1.86   The frequency of system inspections should be increased if the water quality deteriorates or there is an incident likely to lead to increased fouling. If inspections are infrequent, such as for a continuously operating system, then precautions need to be particularly rigorous and additional control measures may be required.

1.87   Access permitting, pre-clean inspections should look for evidence of fouling in the following areas:

■   cooling tower base tank (or pond) and other system sumps;
■   the cooling tower pack;
■   distribution troughs or spray nozzles;
■   drift eliminators.

1.88   If the cooling tower sump or pack is heavily fouled, it is probable that other parts of the system, such as heat exchangers and pipework, are also fouled and require cleaning either by physical and/or chemical means. Where possible, a more comprehensive inspection of these parts should be undertaken, eg during a shut down. Inspections should be carried out with all the circulating water pumps and air fans switched off.

1.89   Table 1.3 provides guidance on what to inspect, how to inspect and what to look for in the various parts of the cooling system. Keep a record of any significant findings and actions.

Table 1.3 Guidance on cooling water system inspection

What to inspect	How to inspect	What to look for
General system condition	Visually inspect the accessible parts during normal operation and particularly during shutdown	Damage to protective finishes Scaling and/or corrosion Biofilm/biofouling Build-up of dirt and debris
Heat exchanger	Visually inspect the heat exchanger for degree of fouling and refer to heat transfer data, if available	Scale, corrosion or fouling
Cooling tower water distribution system	Visually inspect during shutdown – (ensure safe means of access). Poor distribution may be evident from deposition or damage to the top of the pack	Deposition in trough or nozzles Poor water distribution Physical damage and leakage
Drift eliminators	Visually inspect (ensure safe access) Where possible remove for thorough inspection	Deposits Damage Correct orientation and fitting
Cooling tower pack	Visual assessment techniques of the cooling tower pack include: ■ removal of the entire pack ■ removal of the representative sections of the pack ■ use of a boroscope to inspect representative sections of the pack either removed or in situ ■ wet weight assessment of pack sections compared to new sections ■ knock out dry sections of pack to dislodge deposits ■ split pack blocks to inspect them internally ■ visual assessment with a comprehensive written and photographic record	Correct fitting and orientation Sagging Embrittlement Deposition and fouling Evidence of poor water distribution
Fill pack supports and internal structures	Inspect these once the pack is removed or assess in another way if the pack cannot be removed, eg using a boroscope or a digital camera	Corrosion Sagging or collapse Build-up of deposits
Fill baskets and tie rods (sheet pack)	Where practical remove, otherwise inspect in situ	Corrosion or embrittlement Collapse of modules
Cooling tower base tank (or pond) and other system sumps	Visual assessment after draining, but a more limited assessment can be made by probing a sump without draining	Build-up of deposits Evidence of process contamination Biofouling

How do I interpret the findings of the inspection?

1.90   Deposits are likely to be comprised of a mixture of foulants such as scale or corrosion products, airborne dust or foreign bodies, waterborne silt from the incoming water supply, process contaminants and/or biofilm. Table 1.4 shows the significance of each type of deposit and the recommended corrective actions.

Table 1.4 The significance of and recommended actions for different types of deposit

Deposit source/ composition	Significance	Recommended action
Hardness scale	Hardness scale forms a barrier to treatment chemicals and may provide microbial habitat. Scale formation results in loss of heat transfer, reduced flow rates, loss of cooling efficiency	Where necessary, clean with appropriate process Review water treatment scale control measures For fill packs, see Table 1.5 for acceptability based on deposit thickness and surface coverage
Mud and silt or airborne dust from agriculture, industry, earthworks, building or demolition	Sediment is likely to accumulate in areas where the water velocity is low, such as the cooling tower base tank (or pond), distribution manifolds and troughs and balance lines. Sediment can provide a microbial habitat and will encourage under-deposit corrosion For fill packs, refer to Table 1.5 for acceptability based on coverage and thickness of sediment layer	Where necessary clean with appropriate process Review water treatment fouling control measures Consider increasing the frequency of cleaning and inspection Consider additional control measures such as filtration
Airborne foreign bodies and organic deposits (non-microbial), eg leaves	These can impair airflow, water flow and cooling efficiency and provide microbial nutrients	Remove as soon as practicable. Review the frequency of inspection and cleaning Consider using more effective inlet shielding
Organic process contaminants, eg oil, grease	These can affect water condition severely and are likely to affect cooling efficiency They may serve as microbial nutrients, form chemical deposits and compromise water treatment programmes	Cleaning should be carried out as soon as practicable Review control measures to prevent system contamination Identify contaminant source to help determine cleaning process
Algae	Algae grow in the light, so they are unlikely to be found in the enclosed system, but they may be found on wetted areas exposed to light Algae can cause fouling and provide a nutrient source for bacteria	Clean using a suitable disinfectant/algaecide and physical cleaning Prevent light ingress if possible Review biocide regime
Biofilm	Thin deposits may be transparent but detectable by feel. Thicker deposits are often grey or light brown in colour. Biofilm can impair heat transfer efficiency, cause severe localised corrosion and encourage the growth of legionella and should be considered as high-risk contamination	Disinfect and clean the system as soon as practicable Review the microbial control measures

How clean does the pack need to be?

1.91 The cooling tower pack can potentially become fouled with a wider range of deposits than the cooling tower base tank and other system sumps, and is a good indicator of the overall system cleanliness.

1.92 After a period of use, cooling tower pack is likely to become fouled and the extent and nature of the fouling will depend on a number of factors, including the chemical composition of the make-up water, the presence of process and environmental contaminants and the efficacy of the water treatment programme in place. Table 1.5 and Figures 1.5 and 1.6 suitably demonstrate the levels of organic and inorganic contamination that are acceptable and where to take action to improve cleanliness.

Table 1.5 Action levels for inorganic scale, dust and silt deposits, based on coverage and thickness on cooling tower pack

Surface coverage	Deposit thickness			
	Eggshell	Up to 1 mm	1– 3 mm	> 3 mm
50%+	Acceptable	Caution	High risk	High risk
25–50%	Acceptable	Caution	High risk	High risk
10–25%	Acceptable	Acceptable	Caution	High risk
<10%	Acceptable	Acceptable	Caution	Caution

Estimate the proportion of pack surface that is covered with deposits and its thickness. If the material appears to be non-biological, anything no thicker than an eggshell can be considered to be an insignificant stain and not a deposit. If the contaminating material appears to be microbial, ie biofilm, irrespective of thickness, the pack should be cleaned. Deposits may be unevenly distributed within the pack, but the dirtiest areas should be used for classification of the deposit thickness. Compare the extent of the deposits with previous inspections to determine whether fouling is increasing.

Figure 1.5 Cooling tower pack photographs

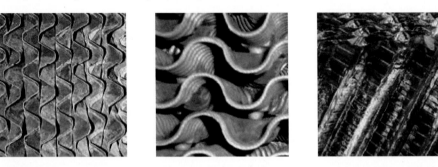

Good: Pack very clean – no action required

Staining and not a deposit

Acceptable: Light mineral deposits only – monitor for deterioration

Caution: Deposits more significant or may be biological – action required

Review scale control measures and monitor for deterioration

Review scale control measures and monitor for deterioration

Deposit may be biofouling. Further investigation is required

High risk: Heavy mineral or microbial deposits – urgent action required

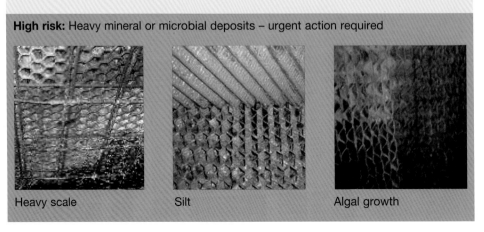

Heavy scale

Silt

Algal growth

Figure 1.6 Cooling tower pack boroscope pictures

Good: Pack clean – no action required

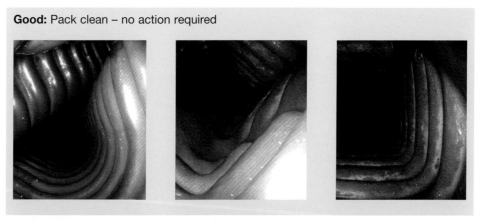

Acceptable: Light mineral deposits only – monitor for deterioration

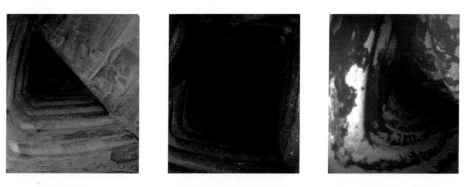

Caution: Deposits more significant or may be biological – action required

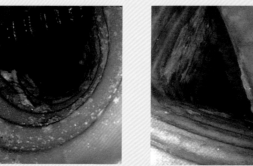  

Deposit may be biofouling. Further investigation is required

Review scale control measures and monitor for deterioration

Review scale control measures and monitor for deterioration

High risk: Heavy mineral or microbial deposits – urgent action required

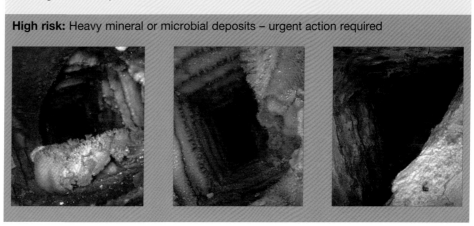

Cleaning and disinfection procedure

1.93 A cooling system cleaning operation will normally comprise a pre-cleaning disinfection (if needed); physical cleaning and, if appropriate, chemical cleaning; and a post-cleaning disinfection.

Pre-cleaning disinfection

1.94 Before cleaning the system, water should be disinfected using an oxidising biocide such as chlorine, bromine or chlorine dioxide in conjunction with a suitable bio-dispersant. This is to minimise health risks to the cleaning staff.

1.95 The required concentration of the free disinfectant should be established and circulated throughout the cooling system for an initial period with the fans off to ensure thorough mixing of the disinfectant throughout the system. Once this is achieved, the fan(s) should be switched on for the remainder of the process to ensure that disinfectant reaches all internal surfaces that become wet during normal operation of the tower and which potentially could be contaminated.

1.96 The disinfecting solution is to be monitored periodically and maintained in the cooling system throughout the disinfection period by adding more disinfectant as required. The normal disinfectant level required depends on the minimum circulation period adopted. A continuous minimum residual of 5 mg/l as free chlorine, for a minimum period of 5 hours, should be maintained, but if time available to conduct the operation is limited, using a higher disinfectant concentration for a shorter time may be acceptable. This will however, increase the risk of damage to the fabric of the system. Excessive disinfectant levels should be avoided and Table 1.6 provides the minimum contact times and disinfectant levels.

Table 1.6 Required minimum disinfectant level for different circulation times

Minimum circulation time	Minimum continuous disinfectant level (as free Cl_2)
5 hours	5 mg/l
2 hours	25 mg/l
1 hour	50 mg/l

1.97 The required residual needs to be established throughout the whole system for the contact time and not simply the cooling tower sump. Systems with multiple sumps may require dosing at each sump to ensure good distribution of disinfectant.

1.98 If chlorine is used as the disinfectant, its efficacy is reduced if the system pH value is greater than pH 8. To achieve the same disinfection effect, its residual needs to be increased 3–4 times, ie in place of 5 mg/l for 5 hours 15–20 mg/l is required for the same period. Generally, this is not recommended, so if the system water is above pH 8 adopt one of the following procedures to compensate, without increasing the chlorine residual:

- introduce a heavy bleed-off for several hours to both reduce the pH of the system water and its chlorine demand before carrying out disinfection;
- reduce system pH by adding an acid;
- augment chlorine dosage with sufficient sodium bromide to change the disinfectant from chlorine to bromine.

1.99 If bromine or chlorine dioxide is used in systems where the pH is above 8, the reserves do not need to be increased or the pH adjusted, as these disinfectants remain effective at higher pH.

1.100 Once the system has been pre-disinfected, the water should then be de-chlorinated and drained. Pre-cleaning disinfection may not be needed if:

■ the system is normally continuously automatically dosed with an oxidising biocide and bio-dispersant; and
■ the control of the microbial activity and biocide residual has been consistently achieved since the previous cleaning operation (ie continuous minimum free chlorine residuals of 0.5–1 mg/l or bromine residuals of 1–2 mg/l and bacterial levels of less than 1x104 cfu/ml or less).

1.101 A pre-disinfection should be carried out if there is any doubt about the control of the microbial activity or the oxidising biocide residual, or there is a delay between the system being shut down and the cleaning operation starting.

Cleaning
1.102 After pre-cleaning disinfection, manual cleaning operations can be carried out with all accessible areas of the tower etc, being cleaned. Accessible areas of the system should be washed adequately but cleaning methods that create excessive spray, eg high pressure water jetting, should be avoided.

1.103 If considered necessary, high pressure jetting should only be carried out when the buildings nearby are unoccupied or, in the case of permanently occupied nearby buildings, windows should be closed, air inlets blanked off and the area that is being water jetted should be tented. The area should be isolated and you should consider other occupied premises nearby, as well as people who may be nearby during cleaning.

1.104 Cleaning staff that carry out water jetting, or other operations which could create aerosols, should wear suitable respiratory protective equipment (RPE), and the cleaning contractor in the method statement should specify this. For example, this could be RPE fitted with filters that will ensure aerosols created are not inhaled. Staff using this equipment should be adequately trained and the equipment properly maintained. Further guidance on why and when RPE should be used and how to select RPE that is adequate and suitable is available in HSG53 *Respiratory protective equipment at work: A practical guide.*[12]

1.105 In addition to manual cleaning operations, enhanced chemical cleaning processes may be required to remove certain types of deposit. Table 1.7 gives guidance on cleaning processes that can be employed for different types of fouling. Once cleaned, the system should be sluiced out until the water going to drain is clear.

Table 1.7 Cleaning processes for different types of fouling

Predominant type of fouling	Cleaning procedure
Silt, sediment and airborne dust (predominantly inorganic)	Physical removal with a 'wet vac' or similar. Post-disinfect to ensure any microbial fouling released is killed. If heavy fouling of this type is 'normal' for the system, consider fitting side-stream filtration
Biofouling	Strong oxidising biocide combined with bio-dispersant and circulated with fans off and heavy purge. Shut system down and drain all sumps, check cleanliness of strainers, heat exchangers and pack. Review ongoing biocide regime
Hardness scale	Acid clean using appropriate acid and inhibitor. If cleaning proves to be ineffective, consideration should be given to replacing heavily scaled pack. Review water treatment programme for scale control
Corrosion products	Acid clean using appropriate acid and inhibitor or suitable chelant/dispersant. Review water treatment programme for corrosion control
Organic process contaminants	Identify the contaminant and select an appropriate solvent/dispersant. Consideration should be given to modifying the cooling system to reduce or prevent contamination of the cooling system water with process material

Cleaning of the cooling tower pack

1.106 Maintaining the cleanliness of the cooling system and the water in it is critical to prevent or control the risk of exposure to legionella; it is therefore necessary to demonstrate the cleanliness of the system including the pack, whether the pack is removed or not. The approach to cleaning the cooling tower pack will depend on a number of factors, including:

■ the nature of the contamination;
■ the design of the cooling tower and practicalities of accessing and/or removing the pack;
■ the type of pack in use, ie block or sheet.

1.107 If a cooling system operates in a relatively clean environment with continuous effective water treatment, it is possible for a cooling tower pack to remain free from fouling for many years. However, a pack may appear clean from the visible surfaces but be fouled internally.

1.108 Removal of the cooling tower pack, where this can be done relatively easily and reinstated safely without damage, will inform the inspection and assessment and aid any potential cleaning. However, whether the pack is removed or not, evidence of its cleanliness should be demonstrated, an assessment made using appropriate techniques as detailed in Table 1.3. and the findings recorded. Photographic records of pack condition can help in this process and should be maintained.

1.109 Sheet pack can also be separated to allow silt or sediment to be washed off. Block-type pack cannot be cleaned effectively by jetting but may respond to flushing with high volumes of water or cleaning fluid. If a chemical process is required to remove fouling, this may be most conveniently done in situ by circulating a concentrated cleaning solution through the pack. Application of a suitable cleaning solution formulated as a foam may remove light deposits in situ. Alternatively, the pack can be removed and immersed in a suitable cleaning solution ex situ. In some circumstances it may be possible to remove certain deposits by removing the pack, allowing it to dry out and then gently knocking or dropping it from a low height to shock the dried deposits off, taking care not to damage the pack itself.

1.110 Where the pack or drift eliminators are heavily fouled and cleaning is not practical, consider replacing them and it may be prudent to hold sections of new pack and drift eliminators on site for use during system cleaning operations. It is important that replacement pack and drift eliminator match or have the same dimensions and performance as the original, as this may impact on the amount of aerosol released from the system.

Post-cleaning disinfection

1.111 On completing the cleaning operation, the system should be refilled and disinfected using the method described under 'pre-cleaning disinfection', using an oxidising biocide to maintain the minimum disinfectant levels and circulation times indicated in Table 1.6. The disinfectant level should be monitored periodically and topped up if necessary to ensure that the minimum levels are maintained. The use of a bio-dispersant will enhance the effectiveness of this disinfection.

1.112 If returning the system to immediate service, the disinfectant level can be allowed to decay over the first few hours of operation and a start-up level of the normal water treatment chemicals added. If, however, the system is going to be left idle before restarting, dechlorinate the water, drain and flush the system and leave it empty. On start-up, the system should be refilled with fresh water and the water treatment programme immediately reinstated with a dosage of the appropriate start-up level of treatment chemicals, including biocides.

1.113 Before water containing high residuals of chlorine, bromine, chlorine dioxide etc is discharged to drain, neutralise the disinfectant. The usual procedure is to add sodium thiosulphate, sodium sulphite or sodium bisulphite as a neutraliser. The effluent from any disinfection and/or chemical cleaning process, neutralised or not, may be regarded by the effluent receiver as trade effluent and may require a 'consent to discharge'. Therefore, permission to discharge may be required from the effluent receiver.

Figure 1.7 Flowchart of inspection and cleaning decision-making process

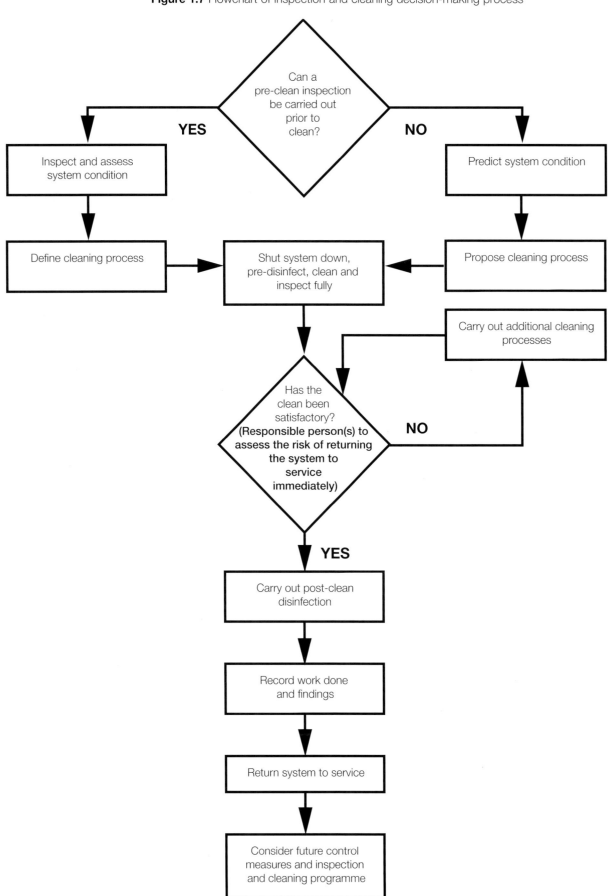

Monitoring water quality and understanding water treatment analytical reports

1.114 The risk from exposure to legionella should be prevented or controlled and the precautions taken monitored to ensure that they remain effective. This section gives guidance on how to monitor water quality in cooling systems.

The need for monitoring and analysis

1.115 The composition of make-up and cooling waters should be routinely analysed to ensure the continued effectiveness and suitability of the treatment programme. There may be more than one source of make-up water. Analyse each one and calculate its contribution to the total make-up. The frequency and extent of any analysis will depend on the operating characteristics of the system. The typical frequency is once a week to ensure that chemical dosage and system water bleed rates are correct. Table 1.8 gives the typical on-site monitoring and analytical checks for water cooling treatment and these can be carried out by the competent site personnel or by a water treatment company.

1.116 The identification of changes in the water chemistry such as pH, dissolved and suspended solids, hardness, chloride and alkalinity should allow any necessary corrective actions to be taken to the treatment programme or system operating conditions. In addition, levels of treatment chemicals should be measured such as scale and corrosion inhibitors and oxidising biocides. Circulating levels of non-oxidising biocides may be difficult to measure but the quantity added to the systems should be checked and recorded weekly. Monitoring corrosion rates may also be appropriate.

1.117 The tests referred to in Table 1.8 should be provided in the form of a report, in either hard copy or electronic format and will form part of the record-keeping requirements. Figure 1.8 gives an example of report (often referred to as the Water Treatment Service Report). It is important that the responsible person(s) and their water treatment provider fully discuss the report and agree any necessary actions to ensure ongoing control is maintained.

1.118 The monitoring programme should also include the routine sampling and testing for the presence of bacteria, both general (aerobic) bacterial species and legionella bacteria. Since the detection of legionella bacteria requires specialist laboratory techniques, routine monitoring for aerobic bacteria is used as an indication of whether microbiological control is being achieved.

1.119 The most common method of measuring microbial activity within a cooling system is using dip slides. These are commercially available plastic slides, which are coated with sterile nutrient agar – a medium on which many microorganisms will grow, but not legionella. Bacteria in the cooling water will grow on the agar and form visible colonies. Comparison with a chart will indicate the number of bacteria in the water, expressed as colony forming units per millilitre (cfu/ml).

Table 1.8 Typical on-site monitoring and analytical checks for cooling water treatment

Parameter* (and normal units)	Make-up water analysis frequency	Cooling water analysis frequency
Calcium or total hardness (as mg/l $CaCO_3$)	Monthly	Monthly
Total alkalinity (as mg/l $CaCO_3$)	Quarterly	Monthly
Conductivity (µS/cm) or TDS (mg/l)	Monthly	Weekly
pH	Quarterly	Weekly
Inhibitor(s) level (mg/l)	N/A	Monthly
Oxidising biocide (mg/l)	N/A	Weekly
Microbial activity (cfu/ml)	Quarterly	Weekly
Legionella analysis	N/A	Quarterly
Total iron (mg/l Fe)	Quarterly	Monthly
Chloride (mg/l Cl)	Monthly	Monthly
Concentration factor (calculated value)	N/A	Monthly
Calcium balance (calculated value)	N/A	Monthly

*An explanation of the terms used in the 'parameter' column is provided in Info Box 1.6. These parameters are typically required to check that the correct level of each treatment chemical is applied and that adequate control is maintained over scaling, corrosion and microbial activity. They are not universally applicable and tests may be omitted or added to, as appropriate, for the specific cooling system, make-up and system water character and the water treatment techniques employed

1.120 Dip slides should be used to sample the system water downstream of the heat source. The water sample is usually taken from the return line to the tower. If a sample point is used, it is important to flush it to ensure a representative sample before the slide is dipped. The dip slide should be placed into its sterile container and into an incubator for a minimum of 48 hours, usually set at 30°C. The incubation period and the temperature should be the same each time the test is performed.

1.121 Cooling system water should be tested weekly, using dip slides (or similar). The timing of dip slides and other microbial sampling is important. The sampling point should be remote from the biocide dosing point and for biocides, which are applied in a shot dose, sampling should be taken when the residual biocide is at its lowest and ideally performed at the same time each week. Table 1.9 lists guide values for the general microbial activity and the appropriate action to take.

1.122 While the number of microorganisms is itself important, it is also necessary to monitor any changes from week to week, particularly if there are any increases in the numbers of microorganisms detected. This should always result in a review of the system and the control strategies. A graphical representation of these data will often help to monitor any trends.

1.123 If the control strategy is effective, the dip slide counts should reflect a system under control. If an unusually high result is obtained, the test should be repeated immediately and, if confirmed, appropriate action taken. Consistently high microbial counts using dip slides should be checked by laboratory-based TVCs. The laboratory performing the tests should be accredited by the United Kingdom Accreditation Service (UKAS), see 'Further sources of information'.

Table 1.9 Comments and action levels in response to general microbial counts, eg dip slide results

Aerobic count cfu/ml and dip slide appearance at 30°C for 48 hours incubation	Typical dipslide appearance	Comments and action required
Less than 10 000 ˙ (1 x 10⁴) cfu/ml		**System under control: Good general microbial control and no action required**
More than 10 000 (1 x 10⁴) cfu/ml and up to 100 000 (1 x 10⁵) cfu/ml		**Caution: Review programme operation** Ensure the water treatment programme and system operation is operating correctly. Adjust the biocide dosage if appropriate and resample after 24 hours
More than 100 000 (1 x 10⁵) cfu/ml		**Action: Review programme operation and implement corrective action** As a precaution, the system should be shot dosed with an appropriate biocide or the level of continuous dosage of biocide should be increased. The system should then be resampled after 24 hours to determine the effectiveness of the corrective action. If the high count persists, the control measures should be reviewed and the risk assessed to identify any necessary remedial actions

1.124 Alternative techniques for determining microbial activity have been developed for on-site use. It is important that the data from such tests can be properly interpreted, so that appropriate action levels can be set to enable informed decisions on the control measures needed. This may be achieved by running the tests in parallel with traditional culture-based methods, such as dip slides, for a period.

Monitoring for legionella

1.125 Routine monitoring, specifically for the presence of legionella, should be undertaken at least quarterly. Table 1.10 gives guidance on the interpretation of legionella results and recommended actions.

1.126 More frequent sampling may be necessary for other reasons, such as:

■ to help identify possible sources of the bacteria during outbreaks of legionnaires' disease;

■ when commissioning a system and establishing a new or modified treatment programme – for which sampling should be initially be carried out weekly and the frequency reviewed when it can be shown that the system is under control;

■ if a legionella-positive sample is found, more frequent samples may be required as part of the review of the system risk assessment, to help establish the source of the contamination and when the system is back under control (see Table 1.10);

■ the risk assessment indicates more frequent sampling is required, eg close vicinity of susceptible populations.

1.127 The sampling method should be in accordance with BS 7592 *Sampling for legionella bacteria in water systems. Code of practice*[13] and the biocide neutralised where possible. Neutralisation can be difficult when non-oxidising biocides are in use. It is important that samples reach the laboratory without delay, and that laboratory staff are informed of whether neutralisation has been possible or active biocide is likely to remain in the sample. As non-oxidising biocides are applied in shot dosages, where possible, the water sample should be taken immediately before an application of biocide to minimise the impact of the biocide on the test result.

1.128 Samples should be taken from the circulating water system near to and downstream of the heat source. They should be tested by a laboratory accredited through UKAS to EN ISO 17025 *General requirements for the competence of testing and calibration laboratories*.[14] Testing for Legionella by culture should be done in accordance with BS 6068-4.12/ISO 11731 *Water quality. Microbiological methods. Detection and enumeration of Legionella*.[15] The laboratory should also apply a minimum theoretical mathematical detection limit which is usually that of less than, or equal to, 100 legionella per litre of sample for culture-based methods.

1.129 Legionella are commonly found in almost all natural water sources, albeit in low numbers, so sampling of water systems and services may often yield positive results and the interpretation of the results of any case of sampling should be carried out by experienced microbiologists. Failure to detect legionella should not lead to relaxation of control measures and monitoring. Neither should monitoring for the presence of legionella in a cooling system be used as a substitute in any way for vigilance with control strategies and those measures identified in the risk assessment.

Table 1.11 Comments and action levels in response to legionella analysis results

Legionella cfu/litre	Comments and action required
Not detected or up to 100	'Not detected' does not mean 'not present' or that there is no risk. Focus on maintaining control measures, particularly keeping the general aerobic count (Table 1.9) less than 1×10^4 cfu/ml
>100 and up to 1000	Low-level legionella count detected. This may be a sporadic result or could indicate a persistent problem (Table 1.2). Reassess the control programme and the general aerobic count (Table 1.9). Ensure the water treatment system is operating correctly. Adjust the biocide dosage if the general aerobic count does not indicate good control (less than 1×10^4 cfu/ml). Resample to verify the initial result and then again to check that remedial actions are effective
> 1000 or persistent low-level results	Immediate action required. Resample and as a precautionary measure, shot dose the water system with an appropriate biocide or increase the level of continuous dosage of biocide. Reassess the entire control programme and take any corrective actions. Resample the system to verify the count and to determine the effectiveness of the corrective action, resample again within 48 hours. If the high legionella counts persists, review the risk assessment to identify further remedial actions

Once the water system is colonised with legionella, it may prove extremely difficult to reduce numbers to undetectable levels and periodic positive legionella results may recur. Under such circumstances steps should be taken to make sure the risk assessment reflects this and control measures should be devised to ensure that, although likely to be present at low levels, legionella cannot multiply to dangerous levels

Info box 1.6: Key terms used in a water treatment service report

It is convention to express hardness and alkalinity results as 'mg/l $CaCO_3$' (calcium carbonate) to simplify comparison and conversion between the parameters. Other component parameters of the water are expressed simply as mg/l or ppm (parts per million).

Total hardness is the sum of calcium and magnesium hardness, which if inadequately controlled will lead to scale formation.

Calcium hardness strongly influences the scaling and corrosive tendencies of the water.

M alkalinity (sometimes called total alkalinity) influences the scaling and corrosive tendencies of the water.

pH influences scaling and corrosive tendencies and the performance of both biocides and inhibitors.

Conductivity is an indicator of the overall mineral content of the water and its value is often used to set the cooling system bleed level.

Chloride is a corrosive ion, which may need to be limited depending on the system metallurgy. Chloride levels can be used to measure concentration factors and may indicate brine loss from a malfunctioning water softener where fitted.

Iron and copper Elevated levels may indicate increased corrosion rates. Soluble iron in the circulating water can promote the growth of legionella in the system.

Concentration factor (also known as cycles of concentration). This is a measurement of the increase in the mineral content of the cooling water compared to the make-up water. Concentration factors can be calculated by comparing parameters such as conductivity, TDS (Total Dissolved Solids), magnesium hardness, chloride and silica in the cooling water system with the respective levels in the make-up water. Concentration factor is a primary parameter set by the water treatment company as a basis for controlling the treatment programme. A concentration factor below the control level is wasteful of energy, water and chemicals, while a high concentration factor may lead to accelerated corrosion, scale deposition or fouling.

Calcium balance (also known as calcium recovery) is a comparison between the overall concentration factor in the system and the calcium-specific concentration factor. The equation used is (calcium in the system water)/(calcium in the make-up x the overall concentration factor). It can be expressed as a decimal or a percentage. A decimal less than 0.9 (or <90%) may indicate an increased likelihood of scale formation.

Inhibitor A chemical additive that minimises the rate of corrosion or the amount of hardness precipitation, or both. Dosing levels will be set by the water treatment company based on the water chemistry of the system.

Free chlorine (or bromine) Halogens such as chlorine or bromine are used as biocides and disinfectants and are known as oxidising biocides. They are dosed to achieve free reserves, typically 0.5–1.0 mg/l for chlorine and 1.0–2.0 mg/l for bromine. Efficacy is compromised at higher pH levels. Chlorine (or bromine) may be dosed continuously or as shot dosages. Application rates can be controlled automatically by feedback from an appropriate in-line analyser.

Microbial activity is usually measured by dip slide, where the result is expressed as colony forming units per millilitre (cfu/ml). Dip slides should be incubated at 30 °C and read after 48 hours. An alternative rapid monitoring technique using ATP/ bioluminescence may also be used. Results are expressed as relative light units (RLU). The water treatment company must demonstrate that the target RLU level is comparable with target cfu/ml levels.

Redox potential or oxidation-reduction potential (ORP), expressed in mV. The presence of oxidising biocides in water affects an electrical characteristic called the redox potential or ORP and this can be used to control dosage of the biocide.

Bleed (sometimes called blow-down) is the portion of system water drained to waste and replaced with fresh make-up water to control the build-up of minerals in the circulating water. System demand influences bleed rate, eg by actuating a solenoid valve via a conductivity sensor.

Suspended solids (SS), expressed as mg/l are fine solid particles in the water, either formed from water itself (hardness salts and corrosion products) or from the local environment (airborne dust, insects etc).

Figure 1.8 Typical cooling water service report

ANALYSIS	RAW WATER		TREATED WATER		MAKE-UP WATER		SYSTEM WATER	
COMPANY NAME AND SITE					**REPORTED TO**			
					COPY TO			
SYSTEM					**DATE**			
Total hardness mg/l $CaCO_3$								
Calcium hardness mg/l $CaCO_3$								
Magnesium hardness mg/l $CaCO_3$								
M Alkalinity mg/l $CaCO_3$								
P Alkalinity mg/l $CaCO_3$								
Chloride mg/l Cl								
Conductivity µS/cm								
pH								
Copper mg/l Cu								
Iron mg/l Fe								
Concentration factor								
Calcium balance								
Inhibitor mg/l product								
Redox potential mV								
Bromine mg/l Br_2 or mg/l Cl_2								
Dip slides (date taken)								

COMMENTS AND RECOMMENDATIONS

LAST VISIT MADE (date)	CLIENT (Name and signature)
NEXT VISIT DUE (date)	SERVICE PROVIDER (Name and signature)

DOSING CONTROL		PRESENT	FUTURE	STOCK LEVEL
	Chemical A	Present pump setting	New pump setting	…kg
	Chemical B	Present pump setting	New pump setting	…kg
	Chemical C	Present pump setting	New pump setting	…kg
	Bleed	Present setting	New setting	N/A
	Auto control	Site unit setting	Provider's unit reading	N/A
	etc…	etc….	etc…	etc…

Part 2 The control of legionella in hot and cold water systems

Types and application of hot and cold water systems

2.1 Hot and cold water systems are those that supply water for domestic purposes (drinking, cooking, food preparation, personal hygiene and washing). This section provides information on the different types, design and use of systems available to supply hot and cold water services.

2.2 Water systems in high risk locations (such as healthcare premises, care homes, residential homes and other situations where those exposed to the water systems are likely to be at high risk of infection) need particular consideration. The risk assessment should consider both the relative risks of legionella and scalding. See paragraphs 2.152–2.168, www.hse.gov.uk/healthservices/ and *Health and safety in care homes*[16] for more information for care settings. Healthcare premises should refer to *Water systems: Health Technical Memorandum 04–01*[17] (for England and Wales), or to *Scottish Health Technical Memorandum 04–01*[18] (for Scotland).

2.3 Those who provide residential accommodation or who are responsible for the water systems in premises must assess the risk from exposure to legionella to residents, tenants, guests and customers and implement control measures, if appropriate. It is also increasingly common for there to be several dutyholders in one building who may also have responsibilities for assessing and managing the risk from legionella. See paragraphs 2.138–2.151 for specific guidance.

2.4 Within hot and cold water systems, the risk areas that support growth of microorganisms, including legionella, are controllable with good design, operation, maintenance and water system management and include:

- the base of the water heater and storage vessel, particularly where incoming cold water reduces the temperature of the water within the vessel and where sediment collects and is distributed throughout the system;
- where optimum temperatures for microbial growth and stagnation occur, eg dead legs, capped pipes (dead ends), infrequently used outlets and areas of the system where there is poor circulation;
- where incoming cold water temperatures are above 20 °C, or there are areas within the cold water system that are subject to heat gain and areas of stagnation where there are deposits to support growth.

Safe operation and control measures

2.5 This guidance provides detailed information on types of water system, design considerations and commissioning systems to ensure risks from exposure to legionella are minimised or reduced as far as is reasonably practicable. There is also guidance on operational and control measures.

2.6 Temperature control is the traditional strategy for reducing the risk of legionella in water systems. Cold water systems should be maintained, where possible, at a temperature below 20 °C. Hot water should be stored at least at 60 °C and distributed so that it reaches a temperature of 50 °C (55 °C in healthcare premises) within one minute at the outlets. For most people, the risk of scalding at this temperature is low. However, the risk assessment should take account of susceptible 'at risk' people including young children, people who are disabled or elderly and to those with sensory loss for whom the risk is greater.

2.7 In addition to temperature control, eg in more complex systems such as large healthcare facilities, additional measures that encourage the regular movement of water are often used to manage the risk from legionella in water systems. The exact techniques may vary significantly in different water systems and operating conditions. Paragraphs 2.80–2.118 give further guidance on the use of water treatment techniques and control programmes.

2.8 The cleanliness of the system must be maintained, as legionella bacteria are more likely to grow in a system fouled with deposits. In hard water areas, softening of the cold water supply to the hot water distribution system should be considered to reduce the risk of scale being deposited at the base of the calorifier and heating coils, and to reduce the potential for scale build-up within the system pipework and components – see paragraphs 2.72–2.73. There is further guidance on cleaning and disinfection techniques and requirements for hot and cold water systems in paragraphs 2.126–2.137.

Hot and cold water systems

2.9 There are many types of water systems supplying hot and cold water services and these vary depending on the size and complexity of the building. Figures 2.1–2.11 are representative diagrams illustrating the range of different types of system or components and are not technical or design installation guides. Combinations and variations are possible, but these systems are broadly grouped as:

- **smaller hot and cold water systems**, eg directly fed mains cold water to outlets with localised point of use (POU) water heaters;
- **gravity-fed cold water systems** incorporating storage tanks (cisterns) and larger water heaters (calorifiers) for the provision of hot water. Hot water systems (HWS) typically operate without secondary hot water recirculation in smaller premises and with recirculation in larger premises. Cold water distribution systems (CWDS) do not normally recirculate cold water and require outlets to be operated to prevent stagnation in adjacent parts of the system;
- **pressurised systems** that can be directly mains fed or incorporate storage and booster pumps supplying cold water and unvented water heaters with or without secondary recirculation.

Smaller hot and cold water systems

2.10 These systems are typically found in smaller buildings such as domestic dwellings and small office buildings where cold water outlets are fed directly from the water supply without storage. Combination boilers or instantaneous water heaters (see Figure 2.1) provide hot water directly from the cold water supply by heating the water as it passes through the heater. These units supply continuous hot water at a rate that is usually limited by their power rating. High flow rates through the units can result in warm water leaving the heater before reaching the target temperature.

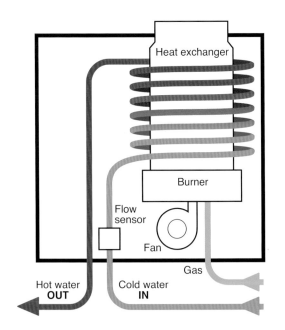

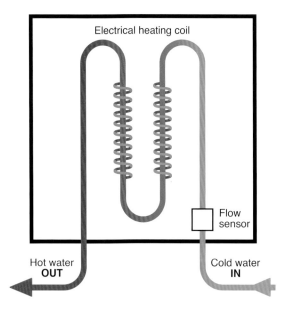

Combination boiler

Instantaneous water heater

Figure 2.1 Non-storage water heaters

2.11 Low storage volume POU water heaters are those that store no more than 15 litres of hot water (see Figure 2.2). These systems generally heat water to a set point that is often variable via a simple dial on the unit. These systems deliver a small volume of stored hot water before they need to be left to recover and bring the temperatures back to the set point.

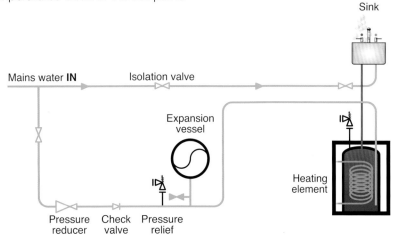

Figure 2.2 Low storage volume POU water heater

2.12 Combination water heaters store a volume of cold water (ranging from 10–200 litres) above the hot water storage unit (ranging from 15–150 litres). In these units (see Figure 2.3) the cold water header tank feeds the hot water storage vessel as hot water is drawn from the system on demand. The cold water header tank is topped up directly from the cold water supply, usually via a float-operated valve. The combination water heater is usually fitted with an expansion pipe so that any expanding hot water returns into the cold water header tank. Expansion may also occur by the cold feed pipe.

2.13 The design of a combination water heater may allow hot water to enter the cold water space. The Water Supply (Water Fittings) Regulations 1999,[19] the Scottish Water Byelaws 2004,[20] and BS 3198 *Specification for copper hot water storage combination units for domestic purposes*[21] recognise this and permit a maximum cold water storage temperature of 25 °C where it is serving other domestic outlets or 38 °C when serving the hot water vessel only. Careful consideration should be given to managing the risks from these types of systems and this should be reflected in the risk assessment. The thermostat should be set to as close to 60 °C as is practicable without exceeding it and hot water at the outlets should be at a minimum of 50 °C; correct setting of the thermostat and regular water usage is necessary to keep the temperature increase in the cold water to a minimum. Where this is not possible, eg during periods of low usage such as overnight or at weekends, fitting a timer which switches off the immersion heater may prove effective. The timer should be set to switch the immersion heater on again in time to ensure the water is heated sufficiently to achieve microbial control before use.

2.14 Electrical immersion heaters usually heat combination heaters but some units incorporate internal coils for primary boiler heating circuits.

2.15 In some combination units, the header tank is split into two sections: one feeding the water heater below and the other supplying cold water to the closed heating system. Possible cross-contamination and poor temperatures should be considered as part of the risk assessment.

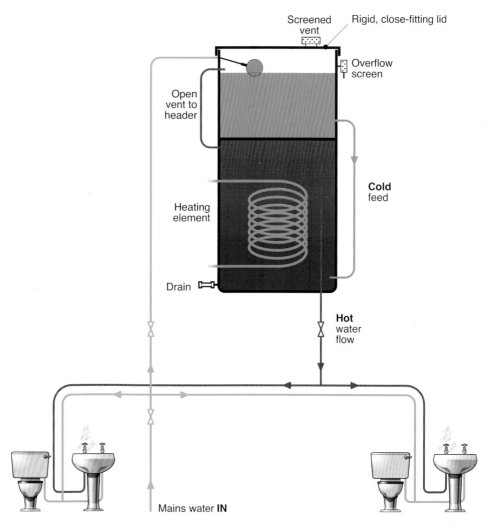

Figure 2.3 Combination water heater

Gravity-fed water systems

Gravity system without recirculation

2.16 Gravity systems without recirculation (Figure 2.4) are generally installed in domestic dwellings and small buildings. Cold water enters the building from a rising main and is stored in a cold water tank. The cold water tank provides backflow protection to the mains supply and a stable pressure and reserve in the system if the mains pressure fails or demand exceeds the capacity of the mains supply. Cold water from the tank is fed to the calorifier (hot water cylinder) where it is heated and drawn via pipes that branch to sinks, washbasins, baths, showers etc. In contrast to recirculating systems, the water only flows when it is being used and is usually allowed to become cool in the pipes after use.

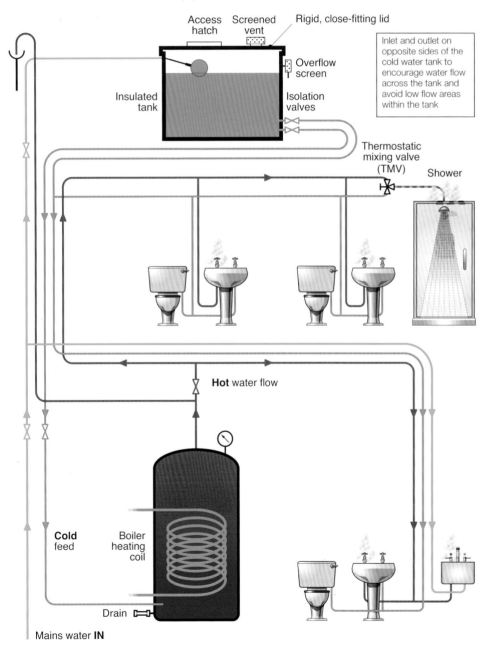

Figure 2.4 Gravity-fed hot and cold water system without recirculation

Gravity system with recirculation

2.17 Gravity systems with recirculation are typically installed in larger buildings such as commercial premises (Figure 2.5). Cold water enters the building from a rising main and is stored in a cold water storage tank or tanks. The tank provides backflow protection to the mains supply and a stable pressure in the system; it also provides a reserve if the mains pressure fails or demand exceeds the capacity of the mains supply. Cold water from this storage tank is fed to the calorifier.

2.18 There is a continuous circulation of hot water from the calorifier around the distribution circuit and back to the calorifier by means of one or more pumps, usually installed on the return to the calorifier, but it can be on the flow. This is to ensure that hot water is quickly available at any of the taps, independent of their distance from the calorifier and reduces the risk of localised temperature fluctuations. The circulation pump is sized to compensate for the heat losses from the distribution circuit so that the return temperature to the calorifier is not less than 50 °C.

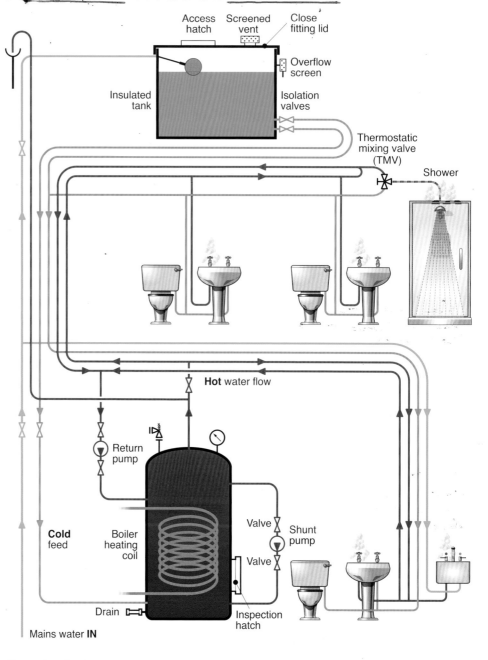

Figure 2.5 Gravity-fed system with recirculation

2.19 The pump has little effect on the pressure at the tap, which is determined by the relative height of the storage tank. The expansion of water as it is heated within the system is accommodated by a slight rise in the levels of the tank and vent pipe. The vent pipe should be directed into a separate tundish/drain which discharges at a safe and visible point and acts as a warning pipe. Discharge into the cold water storage tank is not advised as this can result in warm storage water temperatures and increase the risk of microbial growth. In the cold water system, water is fed by gravity directly from the cold water storage tank to the points of use without recirculation.

Pressurised systems

2.20 These systems are fed directly by a pressurised supply (sometimes via a break tank and booster set) connected to the calorifier, water heater or heat exchanger (Figure 2.6). In these systems, water expands when heated, requiring an expansion vessel, safety temperature and pressure relief valve (in a pressurised hot water system there is no open vent to a high level). Hot water distribution can be a recirculating or non-recirculating system.

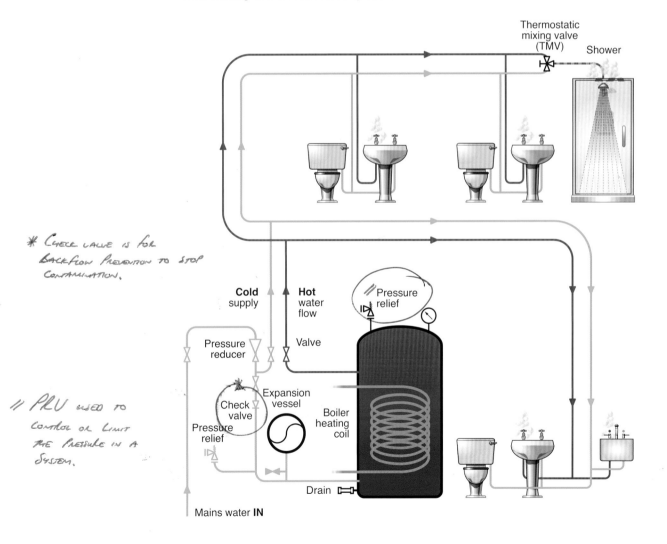

* Check valve is for backflow prevention to stop contamination.

// PRV used to control or limit the pressure in a system.

Figure 2.6 Pressurised mains-fed system with non-recirculating hot water distribution

2.21 Larger systems or those that require higher pressures to reach the top of the building often include break tanks and booster pumps, in place of direct mains water, that subsequently feed the water heater.

Hot water heaters: Calorifiers and hot water cylinders

2.22 There are varieties of hot water heaters available that comply with the Water Supply (Water Fitting) Regulations 1999 and for Scotland, the Scottish Water Byelaws 2004. The specification will depend on the size and usage of the system.

2.23 Hot water heaters are water storage vessels heated by:

* primary heating circuits of low pressure hot water or steam which is passed through a heat exchanger inside the vessel;
* gas or oil flame, directly;
* electricity, normally by means of an electric immersion heater within the vessel; or
* an external heat exchanger (sometimes returning to a holding 'buffer' vessel).

Direct-fired (gas) water heaters
2.24 Characteristic of this type of design is heating from below which avoids the reduced temperature areas found in indirect heating calorifiers; they also have lower storage volumes and even temperature distribution (Figure 2.7). This type of water heater has been shown to have a low incidence of colonisation by legionella.

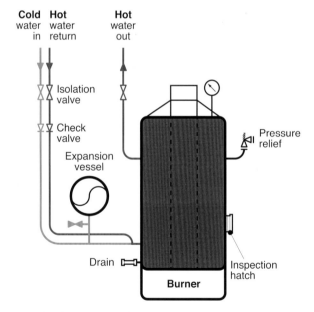

Figure 2.7 Direct-fired (gas) water heaters

Indirect heating calorifier vessel
2.25 In these vessels, the cold water typically enters at the base of the calorifier, creating an area below the coil where the initial blended water temperature may support microbial growth (Figure 2.8). Stratification, which may occur in large calorifiers, should be avoided and fitting a timer-controlled shunt pump to circulate the water from the top of the calorifier to the base during the period of least demand should be considered. The shunt pump should be activated when demand is at its lowest and the temperature within the calorifier is likely to be highest, this is often during the early hours of the morning. The boiler plant (or other calorifier heat source) should be heating while the shunt pump is active to ensure a temperature of at least 60 °C is achieved throughout the vessel for at least one continuous hour a day.

2.26 Ideally, the calorifier will have specific connections for the shunt pump return, as low down on the calorifier as possible. For existing calorifiers without suitable connections, the cold water feed may be used. Shunt pump operation should not be done or any alteration carried out before cleaning and descaling the calorifier, as operating the pump may disturb sludge or sediment. As an alternative to shunt pumps, some calorifiers are fitted with coils extending to the base to promote convective mixing during heating. Particulate matter can accumulate at the base of the calorifier so the design should incorporate an easily accessible drain valve.

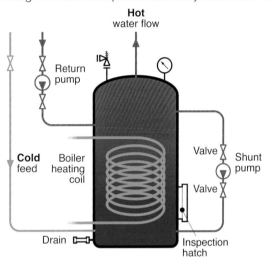

Figure 2.8 Indirect heating calorifier vessel

Calorifiers attached to solar heating systems

2.27 Hot water storage cylinders (calorifiers) attached to solar heating systems or other microgeneration systems (Figure 2.9) often have two heating coils one fed from the conventional heat source (boiler, heat exchanger etc) and one from the solar panels. The solar coil is usually positioned at the bottom of the cylinder and is used to pre-heat the 'dedicated solar volume' – the volume of water that can only be heated by the solar input. The boiler coil is fitted above the solar coil to raise the temperature of the water at the top of the vessel to 60 °C .

2.28 Calorifiers attached to solar heating systems should be managed, monitored and maintained to achieve the flow temperatures as for conventionally heated calorifiers throughout the year. As with conventional calorifiers, there will be temperature stratification providing favourable conditions for microbial growth including legionella at the base of the vessel. However, in times where there is little heat gain from the panels there may be a larger volume at a reduced temperature than in conventional systems. These systems should be designed so that the hot water temperature is not compromised during times when there is little heat gain from the solar panels. If the solar coil does not generate temperatures that bring about thermal inactivation of legionella bacteria; and the residence time for water in contact with the boiler coil at 60 °C is less than that required to effect thermal inactivation, a further level of control should be provided. For example, consideration should be given to programming the boiler coil to heat the entire contents of the solar hot water cylinder once daily, preferably during a period when there is little demand for hot water. A shunt pump may also be used to move hot water from the top of the calorifier to the base, however, it should not be used continuously except for about one hour daily and in all cases the pump should be controlled by a time clock. Where temperature control is not achieved, other measures such as using appropriate biocides should be considered.

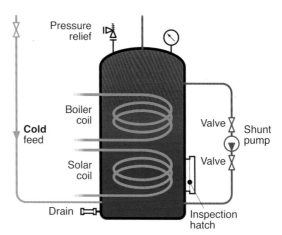

Figure 2.9 Solar-heated calorifiers

Water system design and commissioning

2.29 Plant or water systems should be designed and constructed to be safe and without risks to health when used at work. Such hazards maybe of a physical, chemical or microbial nature such as the risks associated with colonisation and growth of legionella bacteria within the water system. The type of system installed depends on the size and configuration of the building and the needs of the occupants but the water systems should be designed, managed and maintained to comply with:

- the Construction (Design and Management) Regulations 2007 (CDM);[22]
- the Building Regulations 2010 (and associated amendments);[23]
- for systems provided with water from the public supply – for England and Wales, The Water Supply (Water Fittings) Regulations 1999 and for Scotland, the Scottish Water Byelaws 2004;
- for systems provided with water from private sources – The Private Water Supplies Regulations 2009;[24] The Private Water Supplies (Wales) Regulations 2010;[25] or The Private Water Supplies (Scotland) Regulations 2006;[26]
- BS EN 806 (Parts 1–5) *Specifications for installations inside buildings conveying water for human consumption*;[27]
- BS 8558 *Guide to the design, installation, testing and maintenance of*
- *services supplying water for domestic use within buildings and their curtilages*;[28]
- CIBSE Guide G *Public Health and Plumbing Engineering*.[29]

2.30 Any subsequent changes within buildings may result in modifications to water systems that incorporate features from different design styles and materials. Any modifications should comply with the requirements and standards in paragraph 2.29 as if incorrectly designed, these can present a foreseeable risk of exposure to legionella.

Water system design considerations

2.31 The design of the water systems should identify and take into account the following factors:

- the source of the water must meet The Water Supply (Water Quality) Regulations 2000[30] or The Private Water Supplies Regulations 2009 and equivalent legislation for Wales and Scotland and must be wholesome at draw-off points;
- water components that may increase the risk of colonisation, eg blending valves, flexible hoses etc;
- the potential for stagnation leading to microbial growth where buildings are not to be fully occupied immediately or where systems are commissioned as occupation occurs, eg infrequently or intermittently used buildings.

2.32 A well-designed system should incorporate the following points:

- an adequate supply of hot and cold water available, particularly at periods of peak demand, while avoiding excessive storage. In buildings where stored water is not essential, consideration should be given to direct mains systems with local POU water heaters;

- all parts of the system including storage tanks, water heaters, pipework and components and associated equipment containing water are designed to avoid water stagnation by ensuring flow through all parts of the system. Low use outlets should be installed upstream of frequently used outlets to maintain frequent flow, eg an emergency shower installed upstream of a frequently used toilet. Consideration should be given to self-flushing fittings which are validated to show they are effective and do not introduce any additional risks;
- avoidance of temperatures in any water storage vessels, distributed water pipework and any associated equipment that support microbial growth, including legionella;
- single check valves are commonly used to prevent backflow of hot water to the cold feed. These valves should be rated for hot water use, as one side will be in contact with potentially hot water. Where applicable, an anti-gravity loop should be installed in the supply pipework as a failsafe mechanism should the single check valve fail;
- design measures to improve energy efficiency targets and reduce water usage should be assessed at the design stage to ensure the control of legionella is not compromised.

2.33 Materials used in building water systems must be compatible with the physical and chemical characteristics of water supplied to the building to reduce corrosion or prevent excessive scale formation of system pipework and components. Domestic water systems must not use materials that support microbial growth, such as those containing natural rubber, hemp, linseed oil-based jointing compounds and fibre washers. Similarly, any synthetic materials used should not adversely affect water quality by supporting microbial growth. Water fittings and components should be used that comply with the Water Regulations Advisory Scheme (WRAS) approval scheme[10] which lists products that have been tested and comply with BS 6920.

2.34 It is important that there should be ease of access to all parts of the system, components and associated equipment for management and maintenance purposes, eg tanks, calorifiers, thermostatic mixing valves (TMVs), blending valves, circulation pumps etc. Isolation valves should be included in all locations to facilitate maintenance and the implementation of control measures. The pipework and any components should be easy to inspect so that the thermal insulation and temperature monitoring can be checked.

2.35 In buildings where there are those with an increased susceptibility to infection or with processes requiring specific water characteristics, materials of an enhanced quality may be required. Healthcare buildings and care homes should specifically take note of alerts and advice from the Department of Health and Health Facilities Scotland. For example, healthcare premises are advised against the use of ethylene propylene diene monomer (EPDM) lined flexible hoses (tails) as these have been shown to be a risk of microbial colonisation. Such flexible connections should therefore only be used in healthcare premises where an installation has to move during operation or is subject to vibration.

Cold water systems

2.36 The general principles of design should be aimed at avoiding temperatures within the system that encourage the growth of microorganisms including legionella with the following taken into account:

- Cold water storage tanks should be installed in compliance with The Water Supply (Water Fittings) Regulations 1999 and Scottish Water Byelaws 2004. To prevent dirt and other potential nutrients getting in, they should have secure, tightly fitting lids (Figure 2.10). Insect and vermin screens should be fitted to protect any pipework open to the atmosphere, such as the overflow pipe and vent. Where screens are fitted, they should be installed so they do not hold water. To avoid stagnation, where multiple cold water storage tanks are fitted, they should be connected to ensure each tank fills uniformly and water is drawn off through each of the tanks. Access ports should be provided on cold water tanks for inlet valve maintenance, inspection and cleaning.

■ All pipe branches to individual outlets should be capable of delivering cold water at a temperature that is as close to the incoming water temperature within two minutes of running.

■ The volume of stored cold water should be minimised and should not normally exceed that required for one day's water use although in healthcare premises, a nominal 12 hours total onsite storage capacity is recommended.

■ There should be a regular water flow throughout the system and all outlets to avoid stagnation. In cold water storage tanks this can be facilitated by locating inlet and outlet pipes on opposing sides of the tank at different heights (see Figure 2.10).

■ Thermal gain should be kept to a minimum by adequate lagging and separation of cold water services pipework and components from hot water services and heating systems; ensuring higher use outlets are installed at the end of each branch to improve flow; and considering, where appropriate, ventilation of void spaces and risers.

■ Systems that encourage the movement of cold water in areas of the distribution system that are prone to stagnation and heat gain should be considered.

■ All pipework and components carrying fluids other than water supplied by the water supplier and components should be clearly labelled.

■ System components and associated equipment which require maintenance are easily accessible.

■ Water fittings should only be chosen where they are compliant with The Water Supply (Water Fittings) Regulations 1999 and Scottish Water Byelaws 2004. In the case of non-metallic materials, this will also include conformity with BS 6920. The best method to ensure compliance is to select products from the Water Regulations Advisory Scheme Water Fittings and Materials Directory.

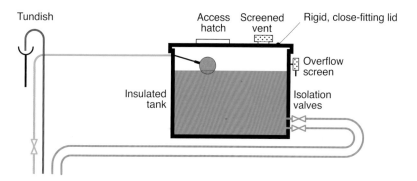

Figure 2.10 Acceptable tank design

Hot water systems

2.37 The general principles of design aim to avoid temperatures within the system that encourage the growth of legionella. Consideration should be given to the following:

■ maintaining a supply temperature of at least 60 °C from the heat source and/or storage vessel (calorifier);

■ the hot water circulating loop should be designed to give a return temperature to the calorifier from each loop of at least 50 °C (55 °C in healthcare premises);

■ appropriate means for measuring temperature, eg thermometer/immersion pockets fitted on the flow and return to the calorifier and in the base of the calorifier;

■ all pipe branches to individual outlets should be insulated and sufficiently short to enable the hot water at each outlet to reach 50 °C (55 °C in healthcare premises) within one minute of turning on the tap;

■ the storage capacity and recovery rate of the calorifier should be selected to meet the normal daily fluctuations in hot water use without any significant drop in target supply temperature. The open vent pipe from the calorifier should be sufficiently raised above the water level and suitably sited in the water circuit to prevent hot water from being discharged in normal circumstances. The open vent should ideally discharge to atmosphere via a tundish providing a safe and visible warning of a fault condition;

■ where more than one calorifier is used, they should be connected in parallel and deliver water at a temperature of at least 60 °C;

■ to overcome localised failures in the distribution system, circulating pump design and the correct commissioning of balancing valves are key issues to ensure flow throughout all parts of the hot water system, particularly the hot water return legs. Balancing the hot water system flow and return circuits is critical to avoid long lengths of stagnant pipework that is likely to be at a lower temperature (see Figure 2.11);

■ the calorifier drain valve should be located in an accessible position at the lowest point and as close as possible to the vessel, so that accumulated particulate matter can be safely drained;

■ all types of water heaters, including storage calorifiers, should be designed and installed so that they are safe to use and maintain, and able to be inspected internally, where possible.

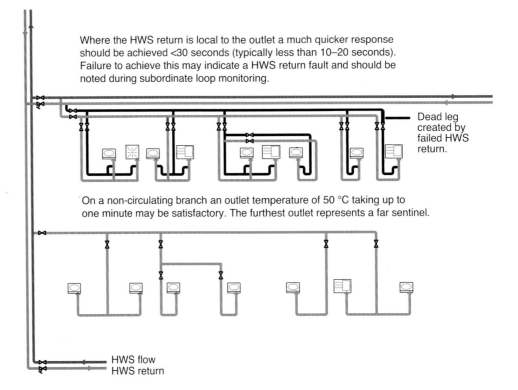

Figure 2.11 Hot water flow and return system showing a failure in the hot water system return

Expansion vessels

2.38 Expansion vessels in systems operating at steady temperature and pressure may have long periods without exchanging any significant amount of water and therefore can be at risk of aiding microbial growth.

2.39 To minimise the risk of microbial growth, expansion vessels should be installed:

* in cool areas on cold flowing pipes;
* mounted as close to the incoming water supply as possible;
* mounted vertically on pipework to minimise any trapping of debris;
* with an isolation and drain valve to aid flushing and sampling;
* to minimise the volume retained within them;
* designed to stimulate flow within the vessel.

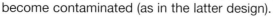

Info box 2.1: Hydraulic accumulators

Where water is boosted via pumps, hydraulic accumulators (pressurised vessels that buffer variations in pressure so acting like a shock absorber) are often used to reduce pressure surges from the pumps and may reduce the demand frequency. When correctly installed, hydraulic accumulators will partially fill and empty between each pump run and should exchange water at regular intervals, which will reduce the risk of stagnation.

In pressurised systems, a means of accommodating water expansion (caused by the water heating) is required. This is often achieved with the use of an expansion vessel. However, these may not fill and empty where the system pressure and temperature remains steady.

There are several types of vessel available including diaphragm or bladder type, with fixed and interchangeable (replaceable) bladders, as shown below. These internal bladders are often made of synthetic rubber such as EPDM and may support the growth of microorganisms including legionella, so check to see if these are approved against BS 6920. Vessels with a 'flow through' design should provide less opportunity for water to stagnate and become contaminated (as in the latter design).

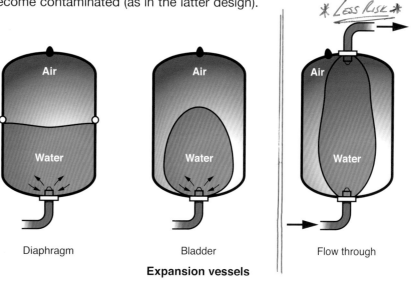

Diaphragm Bladder Flow through

Expansion vessels

Commissioning

2.40 Commissioning of a water system means the bringing of a new system into operation and applies to all component parts of a building water system including attached equipment. The aim of such commissioning is to check the system is performing to design specifications, that there are no leaks and that the flow of the hot water system is balanced. From a microbiological perspective, the period between filling the system and bringing it into normal use is potentially the most hazardous. A risk assessment should be performed before commissioning, to identify and take into account the potential for stagnation as this may lead to microbial growth where buildings are not to be fully occupied immediately or where systems are commissioned as occupation occurs, eg infrequently or intermittently used buildings.

2.41 Any new water system will require, as a minimum, flushing and disinfection before being brought into use, and larger more complex systems may also require disinfection. The building commissioning process should take into account the size and complexity of the water system. A new, correctly designed and installed water system should provide wholesome water at every outlet and where there are any problems, the design or installation defect should be identified and rectified.

2.42 Before commissioning, the nature of the incoming water supply must be determined. If it is a public water supply, the water supplier will be able to provide details of the testing carried out in the local water supply zone in which the building is situated. If there is any doubt about the condition of the underground supply pipe connecting the building to the public supply main, the water supplier should be contacted so that they can carry out an appropriate investigation and advise if any action is required by either them, or the premises owner. If the building has a private water supply, the local authority should be contacted to carry out a private water supply risk assessment, if this has not been done already. The building owner is responsible for complying with the regulatory requirements as notified by the water supplier or the local authority, as appropriate, irrespective of whether it is a public or private water supply, or a combination of both.

Small developments
2.43 Small developments (eg individual commercial or light industrial units, small offices, rented domestic houses) where water systems are simple, should be thoroughly flushed before use, but this should be done as close to occupation as possible to minimise the possibility of microbial growth.

Large developments
2.44 Before use, all water systems should be cleaned, flushed and disinfected as specified in BS EN 806 and BS 8558. This involves adding an effective disinfectant, such as chlorine or chlorine dioxide, drawing it throughout the system and leaving it for a specified time (the contact time) to take effect. It is important to monitor the levels of residual chlorine at selected outlets to ensure the minimum required concentration is maintained throughout the contact period. Where chlorine is used as the biocide, the pH of the water should be checked as the efficacy of chlorine can be adversely affected at pH values over 7.6.

2.45 If water turnover is anticipated to be low initially, it may be advisable not to commission certain parts of the system, such as cold water storage tanks, until the building is ready for occupation. This will ensure flushing during low use periods will draw directly on the mains supply rather than intermediate storage. The manufacturer of any component to be bypassed should be consulted for any requirements, such as whether it needs to be filled or can remain empty until it is brought into use.

2.46 In most cases, water systems will need to be pressure tested with water but once filled, wetted systems should not be drained down as this may not be fully effective and biofilm can develop in areas where there are residual pockets of water or high humidity. Alternatively, compressed air or an inert gas may be used, by trained and competent personnel, to pressure test water systems for leaks.

2.47 If there is a prolonged period between pressure testing using water and full occupation of the development, a procedure should be adopted to maintain water quality in the system. Weekly flushing should be implemented to reduce stagnation and the potential for microbial growth, keep temperatures below 20 °C and to ensure residual chemical treatment levels eg the low level of chlorine in the incoming water supply, is maintained throughout the system.

2.48 In large systems where a long period of time from filling to occupation cannot be avoided, continuous dosing with an appropriate concentration of biocide as soon as the system is wetted combined with regular flushing at all outlets can control the accumulation of biofilm more effectively than flushing and temperature control alone. While other disinfection methods could be used, maintaining 1–3 mg/l of chlorine dioxide is generally effective, however dosing at such high levels may reduce the life of the system pipework and components. This initial high-level disinfection should not be confused with ongoing dosing at lower levels in operational systems where the water is intended for human consumption. National conditions of use require that the combined concentration of chlorine dioxide, chlorite and chlorate in the water entering supply do not exceed 0.5 mg/l as chlorine dioxide.

2.49 Where biocide dosing is used, a regime of flushing and monitoring is required to ensure the disinfectant reaches all parts of the system and is maintained at an adequate concentration level, which should be recorded.

Buildings temporarily taken out of use (mothballing)
2.50 Where a building, part of a building or a water system is taken out of use (sometimes referred to as mothballing), it should be managed so that microbial growth, including legionella in the water, is appropriately controlled.

2.51 All mothballing procedures are a compromise between adequate control of microbial growth, the use of water for flushing (while avoiding waste) and degradation of the system by any disinfectant added. Where disinfectants are used, these should leave the system fit for its intended purpose.

2.52 In general, systems are normally left filled with water for mothballing and not drained down as moisture will remain within the system enabling biofilm to develop where there are pockets of water or high humidity. The water in the system also helps to avoid other problems associated with systems drying out, including failure of tank joints and corrosion in metal pipework. The systems should be recommissioned as though they were new (ie thoroughly flushed, cleaned and disinfected) before returned to use.

Operation and inspection of hot and cold water systems

2.53 The risks from legionella should be identified and managed and paragraphs 2.53–2.79 give guidance on the operation and maintenance of hot and cold water systems. Building water systems should be routinely checked where there is a risk from legionella to ensure that:

■ there is a good turnover of water;
■ adequate control parameters at outlets are achieved, ie temperature and/or biocide levels, and inspected for cleanliness.

Arrangements should be in place for the key control parameters to be monitored by those with the appropriate training and expertise. Alternatively, building management systems are increasingly used to provide an automated monitoring programme, allowing for early detection of failures in maintaining the control regime.

2.54 All inspections and measurements should be recorded with the following details:

■ the name of the person undertaking the survey, verified or authenticated by a signature or other appropriate means, such as electronic verification;
■ the date on which it was made;
■ sufficient details of the sample location so that a repeat sample can be taken at the same location, if necessary.

Supply water

2.55 The water supply to the building will be from either a public or private supply, or a combination of both. In either case, it is a requirement that the supply is wholesome and suitable for all domestic purposes as set out in the Water Industry Act 1991[31] or in Scotland, the Water (Scotland) Act 1980.[32]

2.56 The temperature of the incoming water will depend on whether the supply originates from ground or surface water sources. The temperature of ground water in the UK is typically around 12 °C, whereas surface water temperatures can vary from 4 °C in a cold winter to 23 °C during a very hot summer. Accordingly, incoming water temperature should be well below 20 °C for most, if not all of the year. In an exceptionally hot summer, it may be necessary to review the risk assessment and take appropriate action to mitigate the risk to ensure regular water flow through tanks.

Cold water systems

2.57 An annual inspection of the cold water storage tank should be done to check its condition inside and outside, and the water within it. Figure 2.12 demonstrates the condition of cold water storage tanks and when action should be taken. The lid should be closely fitted and in good condition. The insect and vermin screen on the overflow and warning pipes and any vents should be intact and in good condition. The thermal insulation should be in good condition so that it protects from extremes of temperature. The water surface should be clean and free from any visible, significant contamination. The cold water storage tank should be cleaned, disinfected and any faults rectified. If debris or traces of vermin are found, the inspection should be carried out more frequently.

Figure 2.12 Cold water storage tank inspection

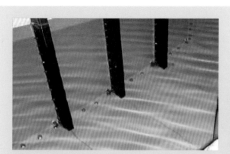

Clean tank but with slight corrosion on bolts

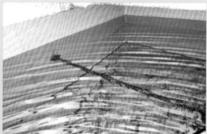

Light debris but corrosion to restraining bars

Moderate fouling suggesting cleaning should be conducted during the next 12 months

Slight to moderate level of debris, tank cleaning should be planned. Hollow tube supports should also no longer be used – see EFA/2013/004 at www.dhsspsni.gov.uk/efa-2013-004.pdf

Heavy debris and corrosion of internal parts that will require remedial works

Severe stagnation could indicate that the tank is oversized, or not being used

Unusually heavy scale formation requiring more than a regular clean and disinfection

Gel coat (glass reinforced plastic) failure resulting in local biological fouling (dark spots)

2.58 Whenever the building use pattern changes, a record of the total cold water consumption over a typical day should be established to confirm that there is reasonable flow through the tank and that water is not stagnating.

2.59 Monitoring for temperature or any disinfectant concentration in cold water should be carried out at sentinel draw-off points, selected to represent the overall building water system. In a simple cold water system, the sentinel points are typically the furthest tap (far sentinel) and the nearest (near sentinel) to the supply or storage tank. In deciding which outlets to identify as sentinels, the layout of the distribution system should be considered rather than the location of the outlet. More complex systems are likely to have several far sentinels, such as the extremity of each of several risers or down services. Any parts of the system not represented by far and near sentinels should be identified and additional outlets selected for monitoring that represent the excluded section.

2.60 Maintaining regular movement of cold water in sections prone to stagnation and guarding against excessive heat gain by using insulation on the cold water tanks and pipework is the most effective legionella control measure in CWDS. For most buildings, carrying out these measures is all that is required.

Hot water systems

2.61 Where standby units are provided, procedures should be in place to allow these units to be incorporated into routine use safely. Standby pumps should be used at least once each week to avoid water stagnation, and standby calorifiers need a suitable procedure to ensure the risk is controlled before they are brought back into service.

Non-circulating HWS
2.62 Monitoring temperature or any other control measure in hot water should be conducted at sentinel points, specifically selected to represent the condition of water in the system. In a non-circulating (single pipe) HWS, the sentinel points would typically be the taps furthest (far sentinel) and the nearest (near sentinel) to the hot water heater (calorifier). In branched systems, the outlets at the ends of significant spurs should be identified as additional far sentinel points. In either case, the layout of the distribution system should be considered rather than the location of the outlet, as they might not correspond.

Circulating HWS principal loops
2.63 In circulating systems the far sentinels are the return legs at a point towards the end of the recirculating loop. Where the system consists of several recirculating loops (demonstrated in Appendix 4), the end of each should be identified as far sentinel points for monthly monitoring. In either case, the layout of the distribution system should be considered rather than the location of the outlets, as they might not correspond.

Subordinate and tertiary HWS loops
2.64 Many larger circulating HWS have additional loops consisting of a smaller bore pipe branching from the flow leg of a principal loop to supply a group of outlets and connecting back to the return leg. In systems such as this, the smaller bore loops are the subordinate loops and the larger loops are the principal loops. Subordinate loops should be monitored ideally at a suitable return leg or from a representative outlet, in order to test all subordinate loops quarterly. However, large and complex HWS, eg in hospitals, often have localised loops that feed only one or two outlets and these can be identified as tertiary loops (demonstrated in Appendix 5).

Temperature profiling (representative outlet temperature monitoring)

2.65 Temperature profiling is a useful tool to verify a water distribution system is maintaining temperatures in all parts of the system in normal use, to control adequately any microbial growth, including legionellae. Rationalising the choice of where to monitor complex systems requires considering the layout to identify the principal loops. These are typically relatively few in number and will take hot water to and from parts of the building, eg toilets or other facilities, and will be one above another in a multi-storey building supplied by a vertical flow and return loop (often in a service void known as a riser and sometimes with access doors on each storey). In lower rise large buildings, the principal loops could run horizontally, typically above false ceilings in corridors.

2.66 As it may be impractical to monitor every part of a complex system, some form of rationalisation and prioritisation should be applied. As with cold water systems, any parts of the system not represented by sentinels should be identified, and additional outlets selected for less frequent monitoring to create a temperature profile of the whole system over a defined time.

2.67 HWS which supply outlets to high-risk users and incorporate tertiary loops, eg showers in healthcare premises, should be identified as areas for additional temperature monitoring.

Low storage volume heaters

2.68 Low storage volume heaters (ie no greater than 15 litres) such as instantaneous units and POU heaters, may be generally regarded as lower risk.

Info box 2.2: Low-risk systems

An example of a low-risk situation:

- in a small building without people especially 'at risk' from legionella bacteria;
- where daily water usage is inevitable and sufficient to turn over the entire system;
- where cold water comes directly from a wholesome mains supply (no stored water tanks);
- where hot water is fed from instantaneous heaters or low storage volume water heaters (supplying outlets at 50 °C);
- where the only outlets are toilets and hand washbasins (no showers).

2.69 Low storage volume heaters serving hot water outlets should be able to achieve a peak temperature of 50–60 °C and where the thermostat is set at these temperatures for this purpose, staff and other users should be informed not to adjust the heater. A unit which is not capable of achieving this, eg a preset thermostat, should only be used where there is a very high turnover or an alternative control measure is in place.

2.70 Low storage volume heaters, which includes electric showers, often have spray nozzle outlets and these should be inspected, cleaned and descaled as part of the showerhead and hose cleaning regime.

2.71 If these units are not regularly used or set to supply warm water, the risk from legionella is likely to increase dramatically and may increase further, where the units are supplied from a cold water storage tank. The risk assessment should take into account the usage of the units, the susceptibility of those using the units and include a suitable monitoring regime where the risk is considered significant.

Maintenance

Water softening

2.72 Light scale formation on the inner surfaces of pipes can be protective against the leaching of metals such as lead or copper, but heavier deposits are likely in hard water areas. These deposits increase the surface area and therefore the potential for microbial colonisation (biofilm formation) and can provide protection from the effects of biocides. In hard water areas, softening of the cold water supply to the hot water distribution system should be considered. This is to reduce the risk of scale being deposited at the base of the calorifier and heating coils, especially at temperatures greater than 60 °C, and the potential for scale build-up within the system pipework and components (eg TMVs) which may significantly reduce flow and adversely affect the efficiency of the system.

2.73 System materials need to be of a type that are resistant to corrosion (eg copper, stainless steel) as very soft water, natural or artificially softened, may lead to increased corrosion of the system pipework and materials. Where water softening systems are used, these should be fitted before any biocide treatment application. Suitable sample points should be fitted before and after the softener to allow for the operational testing of hardness and microbiological sampling if contamination is suspected.

Thermostatic mixing valves

2.74 TMVs are valves that use a temperature sensitive element and blend hot and cold water to produce water at a temperature that safeguards against the risk of scalding, typically between 38 °C and 46 °C depending on outlet use. The blended water downstream of TMVs may provide an environment in which legionella can multiply, thus increasing the risks of exposure.

2.75 The use and fitting of TMVs should be informed by a comparative assessment of scalding risk versus the risk of infection from legionella. Where a risk assessment identifies the risk of scalding is insignificant, TMVs are not required. The most serious risk of scalding is where there is whole body immersion, such as with baths and showers, particularly for the very young and elderly, and TMVs should be fitted at these outlets. Where a risk assessment identifies a significant scalding risk is present, eg where there are very young, very elderly, infirm or significantly mentally or physically disabled people or those with sensory loss, fitting TMVs at appropriate outlets, such as hand washbasins and sinks, is required.

2.76 Where TMVs are fitted, consider the following factors:

- where practicable, TMVs should be incorporated directly in the tap fitting, and mixing at the point of outlet is preferable;
- where TMVs are fitted with low flow rate spray taps on hand washbasins, the risk is increased;
- TMV valves should be as close to the POU as possible to minimise the storage of blended water;
- where a single TMV serves multiple tap outlets, the risk can be increased;
- where TMVs are designed to supply both cold and blended water, an additional separate cold tap is rarely needed and may become a low use outlet.

Info box 2.3: Thermostatic mixing valves

Where a scalding risk is assessed as low (eg where healthy users immerse their whole body), type 2 TMVs that can be overridden by the users are required by building regulations. Where a scalding risk is considered significant (eg where users are very young, very elderly, infirm or significantly mentally or physically disabled or those with sensory loss) then type 3 TMVs that are pre-set and fail-safe should be provided (but are required at healthcare premises) and should be checked regularly to ensure they are fail-safe if the cold water supply pressure is interrupted.

Regular flushing of showers and taps

2.77 Consideration should be given to removing infrequently used showers and taps and where removed, the redundant supply pipework should be cut back, as close as possible, to a common supply, eg to the recirculating pipework or the pipework supplying a more frequently used upstream fitting.

2.78 The risk from legionella growing in peripheral parts of the domestic water system, such as dead legs off the recirculating hot water system, may be minimised by regular use of these outlets. When outlets are not in regular use, weekly flushing of these devices for several minutes can significantly reduce the risk of legionella proliferation in the system. Once started, this procedure has to be sustained and logged, as lapses can result in a critical increase in legionella at the outlet. Where there are high-risk populations, eg healthcare and care homes, more frequent flushing may be required as indicated by the risk assessment.

Checklist for hot and cold water systems

2.79 The frequency of inspecting and monitoring the hot and cold water systems will depend on their complexity and the susceptibility of those likely to use the water. The risk assessment should define the frequency of inspection and monitoring depending on the type of use and user and particularly where there are adjustments made by the assessor to take account of local needs. Table 2.1 provides a checklist for hot and cold water systems with an indication of the frequency of inspection and monitoring.

Table 2.1: Checklist for hot and cold water systems

Service	Action to take	Frequency
Calorifiers	Inspect calorifier internally by removing the inspection hatch or using a boroscope and clean by draining the vessel. The frequency of inspection and cleaning should be subject to the findings and increased or decreased based on conditions recorded	Annually, or as indicated by the rate of fouling
	Where there is no inspection hatch, purge any debris in the base of the calorifier to a suitable drain Collect the initial flush from the base of hot water heaters to inspect clarity, quantity of debris, and temperature	Annually, but may be increased as indicated by the risk assessment or result of inspection findings
	Check calorifier flow temperatures (thermostat settings should modulate as close to 60 °C as practicable without going below 60 °C) Check calorifier return temperatures (not below 50 °C, in healthcare premises not below 55 °C)	Monthly
Hot water services	For non-circulating systems: take temperatures at sentinel points (nearest outlet, furthest outlet and long branches to outlets) to confirm they are at a minimum of 50 °C within one minute (55 °C in healthcare premises)	Monthly
	For circulating systems: take temperatures at return legs of principal loops (sentinel points) to confirm they are at a minimum of 50 °C (55 °C in healthcare premises). Temperature measurements may be taken on the surface of metallic pipework	Monthly
	For circulating systems: take temperatures at return legs of subordinate loops, temperature measurements can be taken on the surface of pipes, but where this is not practicable, the temperature of water from the last outlet on each loop may be measured and this should be greater than 50 °C within one minute of running (55 °C in healthcare premises). If the temperature rise is slow, it should be confirmed that the outlet is on a long leg and not that the flow and return has failed in that local area	Quarterly (ideally on a rolling monthly rota)
	All HWS systems: take temperatures at a representative selection of other points (intermediate outlets of single pipe systems and tertiary loops in circulating systems) to confirm they are at a minimum of 50 °C (55 °C in healthcare premises) to create a temperature profile of the whole system over a defined time period	Representative selection of other sentinel outlets considered on a rotational basis to ensure the whole system is reaching satisfactory temperatures for legionella control
POU water heaters (no greater than 15 litres)	Check water temperatures to confirm the heater operates at 50–60 °C (55 °C in healthcare premises) or check the installation has a high turnover	Monthly–six monthly, or as indicated by the risk assessment

Combination water heaters	Inspect the integral cold water header tanks as part of the cold water storage tank inspection regime, clean and disinfect as necessary. If evidence shows that the unit regularly overflows hot water into the integral cold water header tank, instigate a temperature monitoring regime to determine the frequency and take precautionary measures as determined by the findings of this monitoring regime	Annually
	Check water temperatures at an outlet to confirm the heater operates at 50–60 °C	Monthly
Cold water tanks	Inspect cold water storage tanks and carry out remedial work where necessary	Annually
	Check the tank water temperature remote from the ball valve and the incoming mains temperature. Record the maximum temperatures of the stored and supply water recorded by fixed maximum/minimum thermometers where fitted	Annually (Summer) or as indicated by the temperature profiling
Cold water services	Check temperatures at sentinel taps (typically those nearest to and furthest from the cold tank, but may also include other key locations on long branches to zones or floor levels). These outlets should be below 20 °C within two minutes of running the cold tap. To identify any local heat gain, which might not be apparent after one minute, observe the thermometer reading during flushing	Monthly
	Take temperatures at a representative selection of other points to confirm they are below 20 °C to create a temperature profile of the whole system over a defined time period. Peak temperatures or any temperatures that are slow to fall should be an indicator of a localised problem	Representative selection of other sentinel outlets considered on a rotational basis to ensure the whole system is reaching satisfactory temperatures for legionella control
	Check thermal insulation to ensure it is intact and consider weatherproofing where components are exposed to the outdoor environment	Annually
Showers and spray taps	Dismantle, clean and descale removable parts, heads, inserts and hoses where fitted	Quarterly or as indicated by the rate of fouling or other risk factors, eg areas with high risk patients
POU filters	Record the service start date and lifespan or end date and replace filters as recommended by the manufacturer (0.2 µm membrane POU filters should be used primarily as a temporary control measure while a permanent safe engineering solution is developed, although long-term use of such filters may be needed in some healthcare situations)	According to manufacturer's guidelines
Base exchange softeners	Visually check the salt levels and top up salt, if required. Undertake a hardness check to confirm operation of the softener	Weekly, but depends on the size of the vessel and the rate of salt consumption
	Service and disinfect	Annually, or according to manufacturer's guidelines

Multiple use filters	Backwash and regenerate as specified by the manufacturer	According to manufacturer's guidelines
Infrequently used outlets	Consideration should be given to removing infrequently used showers, taps and any associated equipment that uses water. If removed, any redundant supply pipework should be cut back as far as possible to a common supply (eg to the recirculating pipework or the pipework supplying a more frequently used upstream fitting) but preferably by removing the feeding 'T' Infrequently used equipment within a water system (ie not used for a period equal to or greater than seven days) should be included on the flushing regime Flush the outlets until the temperature at the outlet stabilises and is comparable to supply water and purge to drain Regularly use the outlets to minimise the risk from microbial growth in the peripheral parts of the water system, sustain and log this procedure once started For high risk populations, eg healthcare and care homes, more frequent flushing may be required as indicated by the risk assessment	Weekly, or as indicated by the risk assessment
TMVs	Risk assess whether the TMV fitting is required, and if not, remove Where needed, inspect, clean, descale and disinfect any strainers or filters associated with TMVs To maintain protection against scald risk, TMVs require regular routine maintenance carried out by competent persons in accordance with the manufacturer's instructions. There is further information in paragraphs 2.152–2.168	Annually or on a frequency defined by the risk assessment, taking account of any manufacturer's recommendations
Expansion vessels	Where practical, flush through and purge to drain. Bladders should be changed according to the manufacturer's guidelines or as indicated by the risk assessment	Monthly–six monthly, as indicated by the risk assessment

Water treatment and control programmes for hot and cold water systems

2.80 Dutyholders are required to prevent or control the risk from exposure to legionella. Precautions include physical methods such as regular movement of hot and cold water in distribution pipework, regular flushing of outlets to ensure water cannot stagnate in the hot and cold water systems and POU filters. For control measures to be effective, it is essential to keep the whole system clean, as biofilms or inorganic matter such as scale can reduce the efficacy of any type of control measure significantly.

2.81 Although temperature is the traditional and most common approach to control, sometimes there can be technical difficulties in maintaining the required temperatures, particularly in older buildings with complex water systems. Control methods including water treatment techniques, when used correctly and if properly managed, can be effective in the control of legionella in hot and cold water systems. However, the selection of a suitable system for the control of legionella is complex and depends on a number of parameters, including system design, age, size, and water chemistry, all of which can contribute to the complexity and difficulty of achieving adequate control. There is no single water treatment control regime that is effective in every case, and each control method has both benefits and limitations.

Temperature regime

2.82 Where temperature is used, hot water should be stored at a minimum of 60 °C and distributed so it reaches a minimum temperature of 50 °C (55 °C in healthcare premises) within one minute at outlets. Where circulation is not possible, trace heating is sometimes used to maintain the water temperature in the spur so that it delivers at 50 °C within one minute of running, but only provided it is shown to be effective.

2.83 Much higher temperatures should be avoided because of the risk of scalding. At 50 °C, the risk of scalding is small for most people but the risk increases rapidly with higher temperatures and for longer exposure times. However, the risk, particularly to young children, the elderly or disabled and to those with sensory loss will be greater. Where a significant scalding risk is identified, using TMVs on baths and showers should be considered to reduce temperature and should be placed as close to the POU as possible. To ensure the correct function of TMVs, there needs to be a minimum temperature differential between the hot and cold water supplies and the mixed water temperature. Users should refer to the manufacturer's operating instructions to ensure these devices are working safely and correctly.

2.84 When using temperature as a control regime, as well as routine monitoring and inspection, the checks in Table 2.1 should also be carried out and remedial action taken if necessary.

Biocide treatments

2.85 Where biocides are used to treat water systems, like the temperature regime they require meticulous control and monitoring programmes in place if they are to be equally effective. However, in healthcare premises, careful consideration should be given to any equipment that is connected to the water system that may be affected by the application of a biocide, eg renal and haemodialysis units. Due to the extremely sensitive nature of renal water plants, for healthcare premises reference should be made to *Water systems: Health Technical Memorandum 04-01* Part B (for England and Wales), or to *Scottish Health Technical Memorandum 04-01* (for Scotland).

2.86 If hot water is not needed for other reasons, eg for kitchens or laundries, and there is no requirement to store hot water at 60 °C (or distribute at 50 °C), then hot water temperatures can be reduced. As reducing hot water temperatures will leave the system vulnerable if there are any lapses in the biocide control regime, the control system should be checked at least weekly to ensure it is operating effectively and continuing to control legionella.

2.87 Any reduction of hot water temperatures should be carried out in stages and temperatures only reduced when efficacy against legionella is confirmed, with monitoring for legionella and biocide levels in the water system carried out at each stage.

2.88 However, reducing calorifier temperatures to below 60 °C, and using a biocide as the primary control measure, is currently not permitted in healthcare premises where there are patients who are at an increased risk of contracting legionnaires' disease. Healthcare premises should refer to *Water systems: Health Technical Memorandum 04-01* Part B (for England and Wales), or to *Scottish Health Technical Memorandum 04-01* (for Scotland).

2.89 It is essential that these water treatment programmes are monitored to demonstrate that the programmes are working within the established guidelines and are effective in controlling legionella bacteria in water systems. The frequency of monitoring and test procedures will vary according to the method selected.

2.90 Biocides used to treat water systems where water is used for domestic purposes may be contrary to water legislation and may make the water unwholesome. These systems should be selected with care and must comply with the requirements of The Water Supply (Water Quality) Regulations 2000, for Wales, the Water Supply (Water Quality) (Wales) Regulations 2010[33] and for Scotland, The Water Supply (Water Quality) (Scotland) Regulations 2001[34] and 2010.[35] Additionally, the installation of any biocidal system must comply with the requirements of The Water Supply (Water Fittings) Regulations 1999 and for Scotland, the Scottish Water Byelaws 2004.

Chlorine dioxide

2.91 Chlorine dioxide is an oxidising biocide/disinfectant that when used correctly, has been shown to be effective at controlling both legionella and biofilm growth in hot and cold water systems. In the appropriate application, it may be used to aid legionella control where maintaining a conventional temperature regime is difficult or where the removal of all dead legs and little used outlets is impractical. Chlorine dioxide is usually produced on site from a chlorite-based precursor using a chlorine dioxide generator or dosing system by reaction with one or more other chemical precursors or by a catalytic oxidation process.

2.92 Use of chlorine dioxide as a legionella control strategy is subject to BS EN 12671[36] and national conditions of use require that the combined concentration of chlorine dioxide, chlorite and chlorate in the drinking water does not exceed 0.5 mg/l as chlorine dioxide.

2.93 Establishing and maintaining a chlorine dioxide residual (as total oxidant) of 0.1– 0.5 mg/l at an outlet is usually sufficient to control legionella in the preceding pipework, although in a heavily colonised system higher residuals may be necessary.

The dosage rate of chlorine dioxide required to achieve this residual will be dependent on the length and complexity of the water distribution system, the water turnover rate and the extent to which the water system is contaminated with an established biofilm. In a relatively clean water system with a high water turnover, a dosage rate of up to 0.5 mg/l is usually sufficient to achieve the desired residual at the outlets. While chlorine dioxide is not affected by the pH or hardness of the water, it is sometimes difficult to monitor chlorine dioxide samples in domestic HWS due to its increased volatility causing the chlorine dioxide reserve to be lost when taking a water sample. In a system containing infrequently used outlets, a programme of regularly flushing the outlets should be maintained until a chlorine dioxide residual is detected.

2.94 Chlorine dioxide is a water soluble gas and can penetrate and control established biofilms. If a system is heavily colonised then it will have a significant chlorine dioxide demand and it may be some considerable time before a stable chlorine dioxide residual is established at the extremities of the system. During the clean-up phase, it may be necessary to maintain a higher dosage rate than 0.5 mg/l and outlets normally used for drinking purposes will require additional controls. In such cases, an offline super-disinfection with an elevated level of chlorine dioxide (20– 50 mg/l) may be necessary, but this should only be undertaken following a detailed risk assessment and the system should be flushed through thoroughly after cleaning.

2.95 Where some of the water is used for drinking purposes, but the desired microbial control cannot be achieved without the combined total oxidant levels at the outlets exceeding 0.5 mg/l then the relevant outlets should be clearly labelled as unsuitable for drinking. Alternatively, the oxidants can be removed from the water at the POU by means of a suitable activated carbon-based drinking water filter. However, where such outlets are in neonatal or augmented care units, these should be clearly labelled as unsuitable for ingestion, including making up neonates' feeds.

2.96 When introducing chlorine dioxide, the dosing system should typically be installed, for a combined hot and cold water system, on the inlet to the tank supplying water to the remainder of the system. For a hot water system, this would be on the cold water inlet to the calorifier. The dosage of chlorine dioxide should be proportional to the water flow and the dosing system should incorporate safeguards to prevent inadvertent overdosing. In the case of hot water distribution systems with calorifiers/water heaters operating conventionally (ie at 60 °C), there will be a tendency for chlorine dioxide to be lost by 'gassing off', especially if the retention time in a vented calorifier/water heater is long. In most cases, however, some level of total oxidant should be found in the hot water, although at concentrations far less than the 0.5 mg/l injected.

2.97 It may be difficult to establish the desired chlorine dioxide residual throughout all areas of a large complex water distribution system from a single dosing point, particularly if it is colonised by an established biofilm. Installing satellite-dosing systems may be needed to boost the residual at key areas, such as interposing tanks or upstream of calorifiers.

2.98 Excessive levels of chlorine dioxide should be avoided since they can encourage the corrosion of copper and steel pipework and high levels of chlorine dioxide can degrade certain types of polyethylene pipework particularly at elevated temperatures. Users of chlorine dioxide systems will need to consider these issues and when choosing a system these points should be checked to ensure that the supplier addresses them satisfactorily.

2.99 The chlorine dioxide dosing system should be inspected at least weekly to confirm that it is operating correctly and that there is no evidence of chemical leakage. The treated water should be tested regularly at a suitable sample point downstream of the injection point to verify that there is at least 80% reaction efficiency, thus minimising the contribution of chlorite to the biocide dose; and at the sentinel outlets to verify the chlorine dioxide and total oxidant/chlorite residuals are as required. The dosing system should be serviced and maintained in accordance with the manufacturer's recommendations.

2.100 For most systems, the routine inspection and maintenance detailed in the bulleted list below is usually sufficient to ensure control, with any remedial action taken when necessary and recorded.

- weekly – check the system operation and chemical stocks in the reservoir;
- monthly – test the treated water for both chlorine dioxide and total oxidant/ chlorite at an outlet close to the point of injection to verify the dosage rate and conversion yield;
- monthly – measure the concentration of chlorine dioxide at the sentinel taps – the concentration should be at least 0.1 mg/l; and adjust the chlorine dioxide dosage to establish the required residual at the sentinel sample points;
- annually – test the chlorine dioxide and total oxidant/chlorite concentration at a representative selection of outlets throughout the distribution system – the concentration should be at least 0.1 mg/l chlorine dioxide.

Copper and silver ionisation

2.101 Ionisation is the term given to the electrolytic generation of copper and silver ions providing a continuous release of ions in water. These are generated by passing a low electrical current between two copper and silver electrodes; copper and silver alloy electrodes may also be used. When used correctly, copper and silver ionisation is shown to be effective at controlling legionella and can penetrate and control established biofilms.

2.102 The Water Supply (Water Quality) Regulations 2000 set a standard for copper of 2 mg/l, which must not be exceeded. However, there is currently no standard for silver used for domestic purposes.

Info box 2.4: Guideline levels for silver

At the time of publication, the European Union and WHO do not dictate any established standards for silver, as there is currently insufficient data for recommending a concentration limit. Equipment manufacturers generally recommend copper (0.2–0.8 mg/l) and silver (0.02–0.08 mg/l) ion concentrations to control legionella effectively.

WHO states 'there is no adequate data with which to derive a health based guideline value for silver in drinking water'. WHO also states that 'special situations exist where silver may be used to maintain the bacteriological quality of drinking water and higher levels of up to 0.1 mg/litre could be tolerated in such cases without risk to health'.

2.103 Where some of the outlets on the treated water system are used for domestic purposes, rigorous controls and regular water testing needs to be maintained to ensure that the copper level does not exceed 2.0 mg/l as Cu^{2+} and the silver level does not exceed 0.1 mg/l as Ag^+ at these outlets.

2.104 Ionisation systems are typically fitted on the incoming mains supply before water storage treating both hot and cold water systems. These systems may also be installed in independent hot or cold water circuits as well as on a recirculating pumped line treating a storage tank. If water softening systems are used, the ionisation system should be fitted after the softening system to avoid removal of some of the copper and silver ions by the water softening system resins. In hard water areas, a specific electrode evaluation and descaling procedure should be part of the programme as it is possible that the natural hardness will deposit on the electrodes and reduce ionisation efficiency.

2.105 Values of more than 0.2 mg/l copper and more than 0.02 mg/l silver are recommended at outlets to ensure effective control of legionella, and the ionisation system should be regularly checked to ensure it is capable of delivering enough copper and silver to maintain these concentration values at outlets while not exceeding the drinking water limits, if applicable.

2.106 Maintaining adequate silver ion concentrations in hard water systems can be difficult due to the build-up of scale on the silver electrodes potentially obstructing copper and silver ions release. Copper and silver ionisation systems that treat hard water systems should therefore be checked more regularly to ensure that the system is capable of delivering suitable ion levels throughout the system of more than 0.2 mg/l copper and more than 0.02 mg/l silver, measured at outlets. The ionisation process is pH sensitive and dosing levels may need increasing for pH levels greater than 7.6.

2.107 The copper and silver ionisation system should be regularly inspected and its electrodes cleaned as required to ensure that the system is delivering steady levels of more than 0.2 mg/l copper and more than 0.02 mg/l silver, measured at outlets, necessary to maintain control. Water samples should be taken regularly from the ionisation system and from the sentinel outlets and analysed by a UKAS-accredited laboratory to ensure enough copper and silver is produced by the system.

2.108 For most systems, routine inspection and maintenance is usually sufficient to ensure control and any remedial action should be taken when necessary and recorded:

- weekly – check rate and release of copper and silver ions in the water supply and install equipment capable of proportional dosing relative to flow;
- monthly – check copper and silver ion concentrations at sentinel outlets;
- annually – check the measurement of copper and silver ion concentrations at representative taps selected on a rotational basis once each year;
- check the condition and cleanliness of the electrodes and the pH of the water supply.

Chlorine

2.109 Chlorine is widely used to disinfect water supplies. Most mains water supplies will contain a low level chlorine residual in the range of 0.1–0.5 mg/l at the point where water enters a premises. This level of chlorine may not be sufficient to inhibit the growth of legionella within the water systems of a building and where necessary, supplementary dosing with the controlled addition of a further chlorine-based product may aid the control of legionella and biofilm.

2.110 Once diluted in the water supply the chlorine-based product dissociates to form hypochlorous acid and hypochlorite ions. The effectiveness of chlorine as a disinfectant is determined by the chlorine concentration, contact time, pH value, temperature, concentration of organic matter, and the number and types of microorganisms in the water.

2.111 WHO has set a health-based guideline maximum value of 5.0 mg/l for total chlorine as a residual disinfectant in drinking water. However, it is rarely used continuously in domestic water in buildings at levels higher than 1.0 mg/l as this would render the water unpalatable and may lead to an unacceptable level of corrosion.

2.112 While chlorine has an inhibitory effect on the formation of biofilm it is recognised as being less effective at penetrating and controlling established biofilms than some other oxidising disinfectants. Where a water system has an established legionella colonisation, the dosage of a chlorine product may suppress the growth of legionella.

2.113 Where a water system is relatively free from established biofilm, maintaining a free chlorine residual of 0.5–1.0 mg/l as Cl2 at an outlet will help reduce the development of biofilm in the preceding pipework and aid the control of legionella. A programme of regularly flushing the outlets until free chlorine residual is maintained can significantly improve the effectiveness of control in pipework leading to little used outlets.

2.114 Where used, the chlorine product dosing system should be inspected at least weekly to confirm that it is operating correctly and that there is no evidence of chemical leakage. Safeguards should be in place to prevent any overdosing in the system.

2.115 For most systems, routine inspection and maintenance, as in the bullet list below, is usually sufficient to ensure control. Remedial action should be taken when necessary and recorded.

- weekly – check the system operation and chemical stocks in the reservoir;
- monthly – measure the concentration of free chlorine at the sentinel taps – the concentration should be 0.5–1.0 mg/l; and adjust the chlorine product dosage to establish the required residual at the sentinel sample points;
- annually – test the chlorine product concentration at a representative selection of outlets throughout the distribution system – the target concentration should be at least 0.5 mg/l free chlorine.

Silver stabilised hydrogen peroxide

2.116 Silver stabilised hydrogen peroxide has a history of use in the control of legionella in water systems. A silver hydrogen peroxide solution is injected directly into the water system and if applied and maintained according to the manufacturers' instructions, can be an effective means of control. As with any water treatment programme it should be validated to ensure it is effective in controlling legionella. The system should be flushed to remove any nutrients and disinfectant released by the process. Silver hydrogen peroxide should not be used in water systems supplying dialysis units.

Supplementary measures

Point of Use (POU) filters

2.117 POU filters prevent the discharge of planktonic legionella and other potentially pathogenic microorganisms (bacteria and parasites) from the tap and shower outlets. They should be used primarily as a temporary measure until a permanent safe engineering solution is developed, although long-term use of such filters may be needed in some healthcare situations. They may also be considered where high level of disinfection of water systems may dislodge biofilm. Where POU filters are fitted, they should be renewed and replaced according to the manufacturer's recommendations.

Ozone and UV treatment

2.118 The strategies previously described are dispersive, ie they are directly effective throughout the water system downstream from the point of application. A number of other strategies are available, eg UV irradiation or ozone, and these systems are only effective at or very close to the point of application. This usually results in the residual effect not being directly measurable in the circulating system. In large systems, it may be necessary to use a number of point applications of these treatments and the system suppliers will be able to advise appropriately.

Microbiological monitoring

2.119 Microbiological monitoring of domestic hot and cold water supplied from the mains is not usually required, unless the risk assessment or monitoring indicates there is a problem. The risk assessment should specifically consider systems supplied from sources other than the mains, such as private water supplies, and sampling and analysis may be appropriate.

Monitoring for legionella

2.120 Legionella monitoring should be carried out where there is doubt about the efficacy of the control regime or it is known that recommended temperatures, disinfectant concentrations or other precautions are not being consistently achieved throughout the system. The risk assessment should also consider where it might also be appropriate to monitor in some high risk situations, such as certain healthcare premises. The circumstances when monitoring for legionella would be appropriate include:

- water systems treated with biocides where water is stored or distribution temperatures are reduced. Initial testing should be carried out monthly to provide early warning of loss of control. The frequency of testing should be reviewed and continued until such a time as there is confidence in the effectiveness of the regime;
- water systems where the control levels of the treatment regime, eg temperature or disinfectant concentrations, are not being consistently achieved. In addition to a thorough review of the system and treatment regimes, frequent testing, eg weekly, should be carried out to provide early warning of loss of control. Once the system is brought back under control as demonstrated by monitoring, the frequency of testing should be reviewed;
- high-risk areas or where there is a population with increased susceptibility, eg in healthcare premises including care homes;
- water systems suspected or identified in a case or outbreak of legionellosis where it is probable the Incident Control Team will require samples to be taken for analysis (see Appendix 3).

2.121 Where monitoring for legionella is considered appropriate in hot and cold water systems, sampling should be carried out in accordance with BS 7592 *Sampling for Legionella organisms in water and related materials*.[37] The complexity of the system will need to be taken into account to determine the appropriate number of samples to take. To ensure the sample is representative of the water flowing around the system and not just of the area downstream of the fitting, samples should be taken from separate hot and cold outlets rather than through mixer taps or outlets downstream of TMVs or showers. Samples should be clearly labelled with their source location and if collected pre- or post-flushing.

2.122 In both hot and cold water systems, samples should be taken:

- if considered necessary by the risk assessment;
- from areas where the target control parameters are not met (ie where disinfectant levels are low or where temperatures are below 50 °C (55 °C in healthcare premises) for HWS or exceed 20 °C for cold water systems);
- from areas subject to low usage, stagnation, excess storage capacity, dead legs, excessive heat loss, crossflow from the water system or other anomaly.

2.123 In cold water systems, samples should also be taken as required:

- from the point of entry (or nearest outlet) if the water is supplied from a private water supply or where the temperature of the incoming mains supply is above 20 °C from the cold water storage tank or tanks;
- from the furthest and nearest outlet on each branch of the system (far and near sentinel outlets).

2.124 In hot water systems, samples should also be taken as required:

- from the calorifier hot water outlet and from the base of the calorifier, if it safe to do so, as some systems are under considerable pressure;
- from the furthest and nearest outlet on each branch of a single pipe system (far and near sentinel outlets);
- from the furthest and nearest outlet on each loop of a circulating system (far and near sentinel outlets).

Info box 2.5: Analysis of water samples

Analysis of water samples for legionella should be performed in UKAS-accredited laboratories with the current ISO standard methods for the detection and enumeration of legionella included within the scope of accreditation. These laboratories should also take part in a water microbiology proficiency testing scheme (such as that run by PHE or an equivalent scheme accredited to ISO 17043). Alternative quantitative testing methods may be used as long as they have been validated using ISO 17994 and meet the required sensitivity and specificity.

2.125 Table 2.2 gives guidance on action to take if legionella is found in the water system. However, for healthcare premises with vulnerable patients, the action levels and recommended actions in Table 2.3 should be considered.

Table 2.2 Action levels following legionella sampling in hot and cold water systems

Legionella bacteria (cfu/l)	Recommended actions
>100 cfu/l and up to 1000	Either: - if the minority of samples are positive, the system should be resampled. If similar results are found again, a review of the control measures and risk assessment should be carried out to identify any remedial actions necessary or - if the majority of samples are positive, the system may be colonised, albeit at a low level. An immediate review of the control measures and risk assessment should be carried out to identify any other remedial action required. Disinfection of the system should be considered
>1000 cfu/l	The system should be resampled and an immediate review of the control measures and risk assessment carried out to identify any remedial actions, including possible disinfection of the system. Retesting should take place a few days after disinfection and at frequent intervals afterwards until a satisfactory level of control is achieved.

Cleaning and disinfection

2.126 The risk from exposure to legionella should be controlled by keeping the water system and water in it clean and free from nutrients, including those arising from contamination and corrosion; and maintaining its cleanliness. Hardness scale may also trap nutrients, encouraging biofilm formation and so form a barrier to disinfectants.

2.127 Where necessary, hot and cold water services should be cleaned, flushed and disinfected in the following situations, as specified in BS 8558:

■ on completion of a new water installation or refurbishment of a hot and cold water system;
■ on installation of new components, especially those which have been pressure tested using water by the manufacturer (see the manufacturer's instructions);
■ where the hot and cold water is not used for a prolonged period and has not been flushed as recommended or the control measures have not been effective for a prolonged period. For example, this could be as little as two or three weeks, but will depend on the ambient temperature, condition of the water system, potential for exposure to aerosols and the susceptibility of users considered in a specific risk assessment;
■ on routine inspection of the water storage tanks, where there is evidence of significant contamination or stagnation;
■ if the system or part of it has been substantially altered or entered for maintenance purposes that may introduce contamination;
■ following water sampling results that indicate evidence of microbial contamination of the water system (see Table 2.2 or 2.3);
■ during, or following an outbreak or suspected outbreak of legionellosis linked to the system;
■ or where indicated by the risk assessment.

2.128 A suitable safe system of work, or for more complex systems, a site-specific method statement should be obtained before the start of any cleaning and/or thermal or chemical disinfection of a water system. The documentation should clearly define the process to be undertaken and should be derived from risk assessments of the typically encountered hazards, which might include:

■ access/egress, storage and special site hazards, eg asbestos;
■ machinery and equipment isolation;
■ work in confined spaces;
■ manual handling;
■ work at height;
■ slips, trips and falls;
■ electrical equipment;
■ chemical(s) to be used;
■ personal protective equipment required;
■ waste disposal and chemical neutralising process (a discharge permit maybe required from the water utility).

2.129 Evidence of the competence of individuals undertaking the tasks should be confirmed, indicating that the knowledge and experience of the operatives is satisfactory for undertaking the proposed work.

2.130 Disinfection of the water services when the system is offline may be by:

■ **thermal disinfection**, ie by raising the HWS temperature to a level at which legionella will not survive, drawing it through to every outlet, and then flushing at a slow flow rate to maintain the high temperature for a suitable period (the contact time). This method is only applicable to HWS and is commonly used as a rapid response. It may be less effective than chemical disinfection and may not be practicable where the hot water supply is insufficient to maintain a high temperature throughout;

■ **chemical disinfection**, ie by adding an effective agent such as chlorine or chlorine dioxide, drawing it through to every outlet, then closing the outlets and allowing it to remain in contact for a suitable period (known as the contact time). This method is commonly used when it is necessary to disinfect the cold water storage tanks and the whole system.

2.131 As part of the thermal or chemical disinfection process, a service record should be kept of all work undertaken. Any items that require attention or refurbishment should be noted on the disinfection record.

2.132 To confirm effective disinfection, any required microbiological samples should be taken between two and seven days after the system is refilled. Samples taken immediately after a disinfection process may give false negative results.

Info box 2.6: Thermal and chemical disinfection

Adding disinfectant or raising the temperature above 60 °C creates a hazard to users by chemical exposure or scalding. A risk assessment must be carried out and a safe system of work put in place throughout the disinfection process. Signage and outlet warning labels should be fitted to all areas to alert occupants of the building for whom the risk is greater (such as the very young, elderly or those with sensory loss) not to use these outlets.

Thermal disinfection
2.133 Thermal disinfection of hot water services is carried out by raising the temperature of the whole contents of the calorifier and circulating water for at least an hour. Every hot water outlet throughout the system must then be flushed and, to be effective, the temperature at the calorifier should be maintained high enough to ensure that the temperature at the outlets does not fall below 60 °C. Each tap and appliance should be run sequentially for at least five minutes at the full temperature (but not necessarily at full flow), and it should be measured and recorded.

2.134 Thermal disinfection may prove to be ineffective where parts of the calorifier or water system fail to reach the required temperature for a long enough period.

Chemical disinfection
2.135 The disinfection of a water system is normally based on chlorine being dosed at 50 ppm for a minimum contact period of one hour, at the end of which the concentration should not be less than 30 ppm free residual chlorine. However, lower concentrations and longer contact times are considered acceptable, as set out in BS 8558.

2.136 Other disinfectants may be used where they are shown to be effective. Their intended application should take into account the type of system and user profile at the specified concentration levels and contact period. If the disinfectant is for use in water systems supplying wholesome water then these must comply with the requirements of The Water Supply (Water Quality) Regulations 2000, for Scotland, The Water Supply (Water Quality) (Scotland) Regulations 2001 and 2010, and for Wales, The Water Supply (Water Quality) (Wales) Regulations 2010.

2.137 After disinfection, and before the system is brought back online, the disinfectant should be completely flushed from the system. Info box 2.7 is an example of a chemical-based disinfection procedure, in this case, chlorine.

Info box 2.7: Chlorine-based disinfection

Efficacy of chlorine as a disinfectant is pH dependent and pH values in excess of 7.6 should be avoided:

- Signage and outlet warning labels should be fitted to all areas.
- A pre-disinfection should take place if the conditions within the cold water storage tank are so poor that they could adversely affect the welfare of the operators undertaking the clean.

Cleaning:

- Drain the tank to the designated drain, neutralise any residual chlorine if a pre-disinfection has been completed.
- Under normal operation, the float-operated valve is a restriction within the supply pipework and so should be operated fully open, flushing any particulate matter from the supply main.
- Physically clean the tank and associated fittings using a method that does not damage the tank coatings. (It may not be possible to clean galvanised tanks where there is evidence of corrosion).
- Remove residual sludge and water by using a wet and dry vacuum cleaner, disposing to the designated location, and rinse the tank with fresh water.

Disinfection:

- Refill the tank with fresh make-up water, isolate from the mains supply and add the required quantity of disinfectant using the turbulence of filling to distribute it.
- Test the contents of the tank to confirm the required level of disinfectant has been achieved using a quantitative test kit.
- Draw the disinfecting solution through to the water heaters and subsequently to all outlets fed from the system.
- Test key far sentinel outlets to ensure the required concentration is reached.
- Test all other outlets with a fast and simple test showing the presence or absence of disinfectant.
- Top up the tank with fresh water and sufficient disinfectant to bring the concentration back up to target levels.
- Leave the system for the designated contact period.
- Retest key outlets at the end of the contact period to confirm that satisfactory disinfectant levels are achieved. Check concentrations at intervals during the contact period and restore the disinfectant levels if they decline. If the concentration should fall below the minimum, restart the process.
- Add a neutralising agent to the tank and ensure there is no disinfectant before flushing through to the water heaters.
- Draw neutralised water through to all outlets, measuring to ensure the absence of disinfectant.
- Remove signage and outlet warning labels.
- If the water is for non-potable use, the tank inlet can be reopened as long as the subsequent refilling dilutes any neutralising product to insignificant levels. If the tank supplies wholesome water to outlets, it should be fully drained, refilled with fresh water and flushed with water free from neutralising agent.

Shared premises and residential accommodation: Landlords

Residential accommodation

2.138 Landlords who provide residential accommodation, as the person in control of the premises or responsible for the water systems in their premises, have a legal duty to ensure that the risk of exposure of tenants to legionella is properly assessed and controlled. This duty extends to residents, guests, tenants and customers. They can carry out a risk assessment themselves if they are competent, or employ somebody who is.

2.139 Where a managing (or letting) agent is used, the management contract should clearly specify who has responsibility for maintenance and safety checks, including managing the risk from legionella. Where there is no contract or agreement in place or it does not specify who has responsibility, the duty is placed on whoever has control of the premises and the water system in it, and in most cases, this will be the landlord themselves.

2.140 All water systems require a risk assessment but not all systems require elaborate control measures. A *simple* risk assessment may show that there are no real risks from legionella, but if there are, implementing appropriate measures will prevent or control these risks. The law requires simple, proportionate and practical actions to be taken, including identifying and assessing sources of risk, managing the risk, preventing or controlling the risk; and periodically checking that any control measures are effective.

2.141 For most residential settings, the risk assessment may show the risks are low, in which case no further action may be necessary, eg housing units with small domestic-type water systems where water turnover is high. If the assessment shows the risks are insignificant and are being properly managed to comply with the law, no further action may be required, but it is important to review the assessment periodically in case anything changes in the system. However, the frequency of inspection and maintenance will depend on the system and the risks it presents.

2.142 Simple control measures can help manage the risk of exposure to legionella and should be maintained, such as:

- flushing out the system before letting the property;
- avoiding debris getting into the system (eg ensure the cold water tanks, where fitted, have a tight-fitting lid);
- setting control parameters (eg setting the temperature of the calorifier to ensure water is stored at 60 °C);
- making sure any redundant pipework identified is removed;
- advising tenants to regularly clean and disinfect showerheads.

2.143 Landlords should inform tenants of the potential risk of exposure to legionella and its consequences and advise on any actions arising from the findings of the risk assessment, where appropriate. Tenants should be advised to inform the landlord if the hot water is not heating properly or if there are any other problems with the system, so that appropriate action can be taken.

2.144 The risk may increase where the property is unoccupied for a short period. It is important that water is not allowed to stagnate within the water system and so dwellings that are vacant for extended periods should be managed carefully. As a general principle, outlets on hot and cold water systems should be used at least once a week to maintain a degree of water flow and minimise the chances of stagnation. To manage the risks during non-occupancy, consider implementing a suitable flushing regime or other measures, such as draining the system if the dwelling is to remain vacant for long periods.

2.145 Where there are difficulties gaining access to occupied housing units, appropriate checks can be made by carrying out inspections of the water system, eg when undertaking mandatory visits such as gas safety checks or routine maintenance visits.

2.146 It may be impractical to risk assess every individual residential unit, eg where there are a significant number of units under the control of the landlord, such as Housing Associations or Councils. In such cases, a representative proportion of the premises for which they have responsibility should initially be assessed, on the basis of similar design, size, age and water supply, with the entire estate eventually assessed on a rolling programme of work.

Shared premises

2.147 Those who have, to any extent, control of premises for work-related activities or the water systems in the building, have a responsibility to those who are not their employees, but who use those premises. A suitable and sufficient assessment must be carried out to identify, assess and properly control the risk of exposure to legionella bacteria from work activities and the water systems on the premises.

2.148 In estate management, it is increasingly common for there to be several dutyholders in one building. In such cases, duties may arise where persons or organisations have clear responsibility through an explicit agreement, such as a contract or tenancy agreement.

2.149 The extent of the duty will depend on the nature of that agreement. For example, in a building occupied by one leaseholder, the agreement may be for the owner or leaseholder to take on the full duty for the whole building or to share the duty. In a multi-occupancy building, the agreement may be that the owner takes on the full duty for the whole building. Alternatively, it might be that the duty is shared where, eg the owner takes responsibility for the common parts while the leaseholders take responsibility for the parts they occupy. In other cases, there may be an agreement to pass the responsibilities to a managing agent. Where a managing agent is used, the management contract should clearly specify who has responsibility for maintenance and safety checks, including managing the risk from legionella.

2.150 Where there is no contract or tenancy agreement in place or it does not specify who has responsibility, the duty is placed on whoever has control of the premises, or part of the premises.

Info box 2.8: Example of shared premises and responsibilities

A managing agent looks after a commercial building and provides mains hot and cold water services to three tenanted areas. By contract, the managing agent has a responsibility to risk assess and ensure the safety of the water from the incoming mains up to where the water enters the part of the building the tenant occupies. The tenants have the responsibility to do the same from the point at which it enters their premises. All parties should take steps to ensure that each is fulfilling the legal responsibilities for the parts of the building over which they have control. The managing agent should take steps, eg by contractual arrangements, to ensure that tenants are complying with their duties because if the tenant's water system becomes contaminated with legionella bacteria it may act as a reservoir, seeding it back down into the systems for which the managing agent has responsibility.

2.151 Where employers share premises or workplaces, the Management of Health and Safety at Work Regulations 1999, regulation 11 (see www.hse.gov.uk/risk for more information) requires that they cooperate with each other to ensure their respective obligations are met. For example, with regard to the management of the water systems in the building, routine monitoring by any party may indicate possible problems within the building water system. This information should be communicated to enable cooperation and coordination, particularly where another party may be able to help or are contributing to the risk. In such cases, a joint plan can be formulated and appropriate remedial action taken.

Special considerations for healthcare and care homes

2.152 Legionnaires' disease is a potentially fatal form of pneumonia and everyone is susceptible to infection, but there are a number of factors that increase susceptibility, including increasing age (particularly those over 50 years); those with existing respiratory diseases or certain illnesses and conditions such as cancer, diabetes, kidney disease; alcoholics; smokers; and those with an impaired immune system.

2.153 Special consideration should be given to patients or occupants within healthcare premises, residential or care homes where they are exposed to water systems and a range of potential sources of waterborne infection, eg patient ventilation humidification systems that are not necessarily present in a non-healthcare setting.

2.154 This guidance gives information on special considerations where there are susceptible individuals but should be applied proportionately, eg in an acute hospital setting where there are likely to be a larger number of susceptible patients at risk of infection, the organisation may need to follow most or all aspects of the guidance. However, in other settings where there may be less susceptible residents, a local risk assessment will help determine which aspects of this guidance are relevant. Further guidance is also available for care settings in *Health and safety in care homes*.

2.155 Appendix 1 gives information on what the risk assessment should consider and should take into account the susceptibility of 'at risk' patients. Both the relative risks of legionella infection, scalding and any additional measures that may be required to effectively manage those risks should be considered.

Info box 2.9: Patients in augmented care units

Water systems: Health Technical Memorandum HTM 04–01 published by the Department of Health (England) advises that it may be preferable to provide separate small systems, with independent supply and local heating sources for patients in augmented care units (ie where medical/nursing procedures render the patients susceptible to invasive disease from environmental and opportunistic pathogens and include patients).

2.156 Hot and cold water systems should be maintained to keep cold water, where possible, at a temperature below 20 °C, and stored hot water at 60 °C and distributed so that it reaches the outlets at 55 °C within one minute. The minimum temperature at the most distant point should be 55 °C, ie the temperature of the hot water as it returns to the calorifier should not fall below 50 °C. Circulation of cold water and refrigeration should only be considered in specialist units where people are at particular risk as a result of immunological deficiency, eg transplant units. All other uses of water should also be considered and appropriate action taken, as these may not be appropriate in an augmented care setting (eg use of ice machines, drinking water fountains, bottled water dispensers etc). Where required, they should be considered as part of the risk assessment as there is an increased risk in compromised patients for legionella infection to occur following aspiration of ingested water contaminated with legionella.

2.157 For healthcare premises, the Department of Health (England) *Health Technical Memorandum 04–01: Addendum* advises the formation of Water Safety Groups (WSG) who develop the Water Safety Plan (WSP). Although the addendum focuses on specific additional measures to control or minimise the risk of *Pseudomonas aeruginosa* in augmented care units, it also has relevance to other waterborne pathogens including legionella. Info box 2.10 provides a brief summary of what constitutes a WSP and WSG. While not statutory under health and safety legislation, the formation of a WSG

Info box 2.10: Water Safety Groups and Water Safety Plans

Water Safety Group – The WSG is a multidisciplinary group formed to undertake the commissioning, development, implementation and review of the WSP. The aim of the WSG is to ensure the safety of all water used by patients/residents, staff and visitors, to minimise the risk of infection associated with water, including legionella. It provides a forum in which people with a range of competencies can be brought together to share responsibility and take collective ownership for ensuring it identifies microbiological hazards, assesses risks, identifies and monitors control measures and develops incident protocols.

As per the addendum, the roles, responsibility and accountability of the WSG should be defined. The chair of the WSG is a local decision but the Director of Infection Prevention and Control (DIPC) may normally lead the group. The WSG may typically comprise personnel who:

- are familiar with all water systems and associated equipment in the building(s) and the factors which may increase risk of legionella infection, ie the materials and components, the types of use and modes of exposure, together with the susceptibility to infection of those likely to be exposed;
- have knowledge of the particular vulnerabilities of the 'at risk' population within the facility and, as part of its wider remit, the WSG should include representatives from areas where water may be used in therapies, medical treatments or decontamination processes (eg hydrotherapy, renal, sterile services) where exposure to aerosols may take place.

Water Safety Plans – The WSP is a risk management approach to the microbiological safety of water that establishes good practices in local water usage, distribution, supply and controls. It will identify potential microbiological hazards, consider practical aspects and detail appropriate control measures. WSPs are working documents that need to be kept up to date and reviewed to ensure the adequate assessment and control of the risks from a wide range of waterborne pathogens, including legionellae in healthcare and care home settings.

WSPs include the need to:

- assess the risks which may be posed to patients (including those with particular susceptibility), employees and visitors;
- put into place appropriate management systems to ensure the risks are adequately controlled;
- ensure there are supporting programmes, including communication, training and competency checks.

The risks from legionellosis should form an integral part of any WSP, ensuring that there is adequate documentation and communication with the WSG both for normal operation of the systems and following incidents, eg when there have been failures in controls, equipment, cases of illness associated with the system etc.

and implementation of a WSP complements the requirements in the Approved Code of Practice *Legionnaires' disease. The control of legionella bacteria in water systems* for an adequate assessment of risk and the formulation and implementation of an effective written control scheme to minimise the risks from exposure to legionellosis. This should be applied proportionately depending on the setting.

Monitoring for legionella

2.158 The strategy for monitoring for legionella should identify patients at increased risk, eg in areas where immuno-compriomised patients are present, such as oncology, haematology and transplant units. The strategy should identify all components of the recirculating water system in those units and representative outlets where water samples can be taken and results interpreted to determine the level of colonisation.

2.159 Legionella monitoring should be carried out where there is doubt about the efficacy of the control regime or where recommended temperatures, disinfectant concentrations or other precautions are not being consistently achieved throughout the system. Where considered appropriate, monitoring for legionella should be carried out in line with BS 7592 *Sampling for legionella in water and related materials*. See paragraphs 2.119–2.125 for further information.

2.160 Monitoring results to determine appropriate action levels, depending on whether colonisation is local to an outlet or more widespread within the water system, should be interpreted by a competent person. To establish if the circulating hot water or the distributed cold water is under control, samples should be taken from separate hot and cold water outlets which are not blended. This will ensure the sample is representative of the water flowing around the system and not just of the area downstream of the mixing valve. Monitoring of hot and cold water systems where TMVs are fitted needs careful consideration to ensure the results are interpreted in the context of the conditions in place at the time of sampling.

2.161 Table 2.3 describes the action levels in healthcare premises with susceptible patients at an increased risk of exposure. Whereas, in a general healthcare setting where legionella monitoring is considered appropriate, Table 2.2 describes the actions to be taken.

2.162 Where considered necessary for ongoing patient management, POU filters should be used primarily as a temporary control measure while a permanent safe engineering solution is developed, although long-term use of such filters may be required in some cases.

Table 2.3 Actions to be taken following legionella sampling in hot and cold water systems in healthcare premises with susceptible patients

Legionella bacteria (cfu/l)	Recommended actions
Not detected or up to 100 cfu/l	In healthcare, the primary concern is protecting susceptible patients, so any detection of legionella should be investigated and, if necessary, the system resampled to aid interpretation of the results in line with the monitoring strategy and risk assessment
>100 cfu/l and up to 1000 cfu/l	Either: ■ if the minority of samples are positive, the system should be resampled. If similar results are found again, review the control measures and risk assessment to identify any remedial actions necessary or ■ if the majority of samples are positive, the system may be colonised, albeit at a low level. An immediate review of control measures and a risk assessment should be carried out to identify any other remedial action required. Disinfection of the system should be considered
>1000 cfu/l	The system should be resampled and an immediate review of the control measures and risk assessment carried out to identify any remedial actions, including possible disinfection of the system. Retesting should take place a few days after disinfection and at frequent intervals thereafter until a satisfactory level of control is achieved

Scalding

2.163 There is a risk of scalding where the water temperature at the outlet is above 44 °C. In certain facilities with 'at risk' patients this is especially so where there is whole body immersion in baths and showers of vulnerable patients, including the very young, elderly people, and people with disabilities or those with sensory loss who may not be able to recognise high temperatures and respond quickly. Where there are vulnerable individuals and whole body immersion, testing of outlet temperatures using a thermometer can provide additional reassurance.

2.164 The potential scalding risk should be assessed and controlled in the context of the vulnerability of those being cared for. The approach will depend on the needs and capabilities of patients or residents. For most people, the scalding risk is minimal where water is delivered up to 50 °C at hand washbasins and using hot water signs may be considered sufficient, where a TMV is not fitted. However, where vulnerable people are identified and have access to baths or showers and the scalding risk is considered significant, TMV Type 3 (TMV3) are required. Further advice on safe bathing can be found in the UK Homecare Association (UKHCA) guidance *Controlling scalding risks from bathing and showering*.[38]

2.165 Where the risk assessment considers fitting TMVs appropriate, the strainers or filters should be inspected, cleaned, descaled and disinfected annually or on a frequency defined by the risk assessment, taking account of any manufacturers' recommendations. To maintain protection against scald risk, TMVs require regular routine maintenance carried out by competent individuals in accordance with the manufacturer's instructions. HSE's website provides further information at www.hse.gov.uk/healthservices/scalding-burning.htm.

Info box 2.11: Use of TMV Type 3 (TMV3)

TMV3 meets the requirements of the NHS Estates Model Engineering Specification *Thermostatic mixing valves (healthcare premises)*[39] and cannot be overridden by the user. In reality, the chances of a severe scald from a washbasin tap are low and the need for a TMV3 on a hand washbasin should be assessed against the need for legionella control. It is important that a documented maintenance schedule is followed and the TMVs maintained to the standard recommended by the manufacturer.

Flushing

2.166 The risk from legionella is increased in peripheral parts of the hot and cold water system where there are remote outlets such as hand washbasins, and dead legs. Where reasonably practicable, dead legs should be removed or the risk minimised by regular use of these outlets. Where outlets in healthcare facilities with susceptible patients are not in regular use the risk assessment may indicate the need for more frequent flushing, ie twice weekly and water draw off should form part of the daily cleaning process to achieve temperature control for both hot and cold water and/or biocide flow through.

2.167 In circumstances where there has been a lapse in the flushing regime, the stagnant and potentially contaminated water from within the shower or tap and associated dead leg should be purged to drain without discharge of aerosols before the appliance is used.

2.168 For comprehensive advice about the legal requirements, design applications, maintenance and operation of hot and cold water supply, storage and distribution systems in healthcare premises, refer to *Water systems: Health Technical Memorandum 04–01* (for England and Wales), or to *Scottish Health Technical Memorandum 04–01* (for Scotland).

Part 3 The control of legionella bacteria in other risk systems

Introduction

3.1 *Legionnaires' disease: The control of legionella bacteria in water systems. Approved Code of Practice and guidance on regulations* (L8) gives practical advice on the legal requirements of the relevant legislation concerning the risk from exposure to legionella bacteria. This guidance is for dutyholders, including employers, those in control of premises and those with health and safety responsibilities for other people, to help them comply with their legal duties. It gives practical guidance on how to assess and control the risks of exposure to legionella in risk systems, other than evaporative cooling systems or hot and cold water systems.

What are other risk systems?

3.2 In addition to evaporative cooling systems and hot and cold water systems there are other risk systems that may produce aerosols, thus posing a foreseeable risk of exposure to legionella. This list is not exhaustive but examples of these types of systems include, but are not limited to:

- ultrasonic humidifiers/foggers;
- misting devices used for humidifying vegetables, meat and other food products;
- spray humidifiers;
- air washers, wet scrubbers, particle and trivial gas scrubbers;
- water softeners;
- emergency showers, eyebaths and face wash fountains;
- sprinkler and hose reel systems;
- spa pools;
- whirlpool baths;
- horticultural misting systems;
- vehicle washers including automatic washers for cars, buses, lorries and railway rolling stock;
- powered dental equipment;
- fountains and decorative water features including those on display for sale;
- non-disposable nebulisers used for respiratory therapy;
- industrial effluent treatment plants;
- irrigation systems;
- fire, dust and odour suppression systems;
- paint spray preparation equipment;
- tunnel pasteurisers and similar equipment.

3.3 Many of these systems operate at or above ambient temperature, or are prone to thermal gain during operation. This may be seasonal for some; for example, irrigation systems that operate outdoors, so may use water at temperatures that fall within the recognised temperature range for legionella bacteria growth. All have the capacity to generate water droplets (aerosols) during operation and some, like powered dental equipment and respiratory therapy nebulisers, may dispense them directly into an individual's breathing zone.

3.4 The most significant, in terms of risk, are spa pools and the HSE/PHE guidance on managing spa pools, *Management of spa pools: Controlling the risks of infection*[40] should be followed. However, whirlpool baths (baths fitted with high velocity water jets and/or air injection but without water recirculation) are not considered a high risk if the water is immediately discharged after each use, subject to the source water supply being safe.

3.5 Any water system that has the right environmental conditions could potentially be a source for the growth of microorganisms, including legionella bacteria. There is a reasonably foreseeable legionella risk if the water system has a combination of the following factors:

■ the presence of legionella bacteria in the system water, either introduced via the water supply and/or via external contamination;
■ conditions suitable for colonisation and multiplication of the bacteria, for example, the water temperature in all or some parts of the system may be between 20–45 °C;
■ where water is stored or recirculated;
■ deposits and materials that are a source of nutrients for the organism and support bacterial growth, such as contaminants from the surroundings or process including rust, sludge, scale, organic matter and biofilms;
■ a means of creating and spreading breathable droplets (aerosols);
■ the presence of susceptible people who may be exposed to those aerosols.

Risk identification and control

3.6 As with all foreseeable risk systems, there is a duty to carry out a risk assessment to decide whether further actions are needed and to maintain records of all maintenance carried out, together with monitoring results. These systems and any others found to present a risk need to be adequately controlled and will often require a combination of measures, such as regular maintenance, to ensure the system is kept clean, regular disinfection and ongoing monitoring where appropriate.

3.7 Most of these systems are likely to require a supply of mains water and will therefore be subject to the regulatory applications of the Water Supply (Water Fitting) Regulations 1999 and The Water Supply (Water Quality) Regulations 2001. To assess the risk properly, it is necessary to understand the system and its operation. The risk assessment should also consider:

■ the source of the water with respect to the likelihood of legionella contamination;
■ the potential for microorganisms to grow;
■ the potential for aerosol release;
■ the likelihood and susceptibility of people being exposed to the aerosols.

3.8 If the findings show the risks from exposure to legionella are insignificant and properly managed, no further action may be required. However, it is important to review the risk assessment regularly in case anything changes in the water system or its use.

3.9 If the assessment shows there are risks from exposure to legionella:

■ consider if the system can be replaced with a dry system. Where this not practicable, draw up and put in place a written scheme of measures to prevent or control the risks of exposure to the bacteria – the extent and complexity of the written scheme will be dictated by the level of risk;
■ monitor any control measures and keep records of the results;
■ record the significant findings of the risk assessment and keep appropriate records, with an indication of when to review the assessment and what to consider;
■ review the assessment regularly to see whether circumstances that could alter the risk have changed;

- review the written scheme if the level of risk changes;
- ensure that those people involved in controlling the risks (including any contractors) are competent to do so and that their roles, responsibilities and reporting lines are clearly set down.

3.10 When carrying out the risk assessment, the dutyholder may need access to competent help and advice. Unless there is sufficient knowledge and expertise within your company, specialist help may be needed to carry out the legionella risk assessment, and to devise and implement an effective written scheme and monitor its effectiveness.

3.11 A summary of the actions that should be taken for other risk systems is detailed in Appendix 6 and are in addition to the manufacturer's instructions. Further information is also available on the HSE website at www.hse.gov.uk/ legionnaires/other-risk-systems.htm. Additionally, the Water Management Society publishes guidance on a number of other risk systems including industrial process systems, air scrubbers, vehicle washers, emergency showers, dental equipment and solar heating systems at www.wmsoc.org.uk.

Appendix 1 Legionella risk assessment

1 It is a legal duty to carry out an assessment to identify and assess whether there is a risk posed by exposure to legionella from the water system(s) or any work associated with it.

2 The risk assessment should consider all aspects of operation of the water system(s) and, while there will be common factors, it should be specific to the individual system under review. Site personnel who manage the system to determine current operational practice should be consulted. The commissioning, decommissioning, periods of operation, maintenance, treatment and subsequent management of each individual aspect of operation will require review and validation to ensure site procedures are effective.

3 The checklist below gives the most common key requirements when assessing risk associated with water systems based on mechanical, operational, chemical and management aspects:

- Details of management personnel who play an active role in the risk management process, including names, job titles and contact information for:
  - the dutyholder;
  - the appointed responsible person(s), including deputies;
  - service providers, eg risk assessors, water treatment suppliers, cleaning and disinfection service providers.
- An assessment of the competence of those associated with risk management, including their training records.
- Identification of roles and responsibilities, including employees, contractors and consultants.
- A check to confirm that consideration was given to preventing the risk by elimination or substitution before implementing appropriate control measures.
- The scope of the assessment, ie the details and entirety of the plant being assessed.
- Assessment of the availability and validity of an up-to-date schematic diagram, including all parts of the system where water may be used or stored.
- Details of the design of the system, including an asset register of all plant and associated parts and components and:
  - the location of any system;
  - the type of system;
  - the construction materials;
  - the pipework system;
  - details of system modifications;
  - and for cooling systems, details on safe access relating to all parts of the cooling system.
- Assessment of the potential for the system to become contaminated with legionella and other material, including consideration of:
  - the source and quality of the make-up water;
  - the likelihood for airborne contamination.
- Details of any water pre-treatment process such as filtration, softening, particularly:
  - maintenance;
  - effectiveness;
  - monitoring.

- Assessment of the potential for legionella to grow in the system, including a review of:
  - normal system operating characteristics and periods of intermittent use;
  - areas of low water flow or possible stagnation (eg deadlegs);
  - possible process contamination;
  - water temperatures that promote growth;
  - effectiveness of control measures, including chemical and physical water treatment measures, disinfection and cleaning regimes and remedial work and maintenance.
- Assessment of the risk of legionella being released in an aerosol, including potential for spray or splashes escaping from the system during normal or abnormal use.
- Assessment of the risk of people being exposed to the aerosol due to the:
  - location of equipment;
  - numbers of people likely to be exposed;
  - susceptibility of exposed populations.
- A review of the legionella control scheme, including:
  - management procedures for each stage of operation;
  - site records or log books, including system maintenance records; routine monitoring data; water treatment service reports; cleaning and disinfection records; legionella and other microbial analysis results;
  - evidence of corrective actions being implemented (eg defect/action process);
  - evidence of proactive management and follow-up of previous assessment recommendations or identified remedial actions;
  - evidence of the competence of those involved in control and monitoring activities.

4 *For hot and cold water systems*, the following specific considerations should also be assessed:

- quality of the supply water – where this is not wholesome, additional risks and measures to mitigate the risk must be included in the risk assessment process;
- examination of tanks for configuration, flow pattern, protection against contamination, materials of construction, condition, temperature, size in comparison to water consumption and cleanliness or contamination;
- any points in the system where there is a possibility of low or no flow, such as blind ends, dead legs and little used outlets;
- any parts of the CWDS susceptible to heat gain to an extent that could support the growth of legionella;
- any parts of the system with low water throughput including, eg low-use fittings in unoccupied areas or oversized tanks that may lead to stagnation;
- any parts of the system which are configured in parallel with others and where the water flow could be unbalanced;
- hot water system return pipes – stagnation often occurs, particularly at points furthest away from the water heater, where circulation has failed and the hot water has cooled;
- timely, appropriate remedial action to poor temperature or monitoring results and using this as an indicator of the effectiveness and adequacy of the management controls in place.

5 The assessment should include recommendations for remedial actions for the control of legionella where necessary and identify who will undertake such actions. Actions should be prioritised and a review date set for determining completion of these tasks.

6 Further detailed information is available in BS 8580 *Water quality. Risk assessment for legionella control. Code of Practice* and the Water Management Society's *Guide to risk assessment for water services*.

Appendix 2 Legionella written control scheme

1 The risk from exposure will normally be controlled by measures which do not allow the proliferation of legionella bacteria in the system. Once the risk is identified and assessed, a written control scheme should be prepared, implemented and properly managed.

2 The scheme should specify the various control measures and how to use and carry out those measures. It should also describe the water treatment regimes and the correct operation of the water system plant. The scheme should be specific and relate to the cooling plant being operated on site, ie tailored to the cooling plant covered by the risk assessment. Along with the information contained in this guidance, the following list summarises the information to include in a written control scheme.

- Purpose.
- Scope.
- Risk assessment.
- *For evaporative cooling systems:* Notification of cooling towers.
- Management structure:
  - dutyholder;
  - responsible person(s) and communication pathways;
  - training;
  - allocation of responsibilities.
- Up-to-date schematic diagram showing layout of the water systems and their location within and around the premises.
- The correct and safe operation of the system.
- Precautions in place to prevent or minimise risk associated with the system(s).
- Analytical tests, other operational checks, inspections and calibrations to be carried out, their frequency and any resulting corrective actions.
- Remedial action to be taken in the event that the scheme is shown not to be effective, including control scheme reviews and any modifications made.
- Health and safety information, including details on storage, handling, use and disposal of any disinfectant used in both the treatment of the system and testing of the system water.
- Incident plan which covers the following situations:
  - major plant failure, eg chemical system failure;
  - very high levels or repeat positive water analyses for legionella;
  - an outbreak of legionellosis, suspected or confirmed as being centred at the site;
  - an outbreak of legionellosis, the exact source of which has yet to be confirmed, but which is believed to be centred in an area which includes the site.

Appendix 3 Action in the event of an outbreak of legionellosis

1   In England and Wales, legionnaires' disease is notifiable under the Health Protection (Notification) Regulations 2010[41] and in Scotland under the Public Health (Notification of Infectious Diseases) (Scotland) Regulations 1988.[42] Under these Regulations, human diagnostic laboratories must notify Public Health England (PHE), Public Health Wales (PHW) or Health Protection Scotland (HPS) (see 'Further sources of advice') of microbiologically confirmed cases of legionnaires' disease.

2   An outbreak is defined as two or more cases where the onset of illness is closely linked in time (weeks rather than months) and where there is epidemiological evidence of a common source of infection, with or without microbiological evidence. An incident/outbreak control team should always be convened to investigate outbreaks. It is the responsibility of the Proper Officer to declare an outbreak. The Proper Officer, appointed by the local authority, is usually a Consultant in Communicable Diseases Control (CCDC) in England and Wales, or the Consultant in Public Health Medicine (CPHM) in Scotland. If there are suspected cases of the disease, medical practitioners must notify the Proper Officer in the relevant local authority.

3   Local authorities will have jointly established incident plans to investigate major outbreaks of infectious diseases, including legionellosis, and it is the Proper Officer who activates these and invokes an Outbreak Committee, whose primary purpose is to protect public health and prevent further infection.

4   HSE or local environmental health officers may be involved in the investigation of outbreaks, their aim being to pursue compliance with health and safety legislation. The local authority, Proper Officer or EHO acting on their behalf will make a visit, often with the relevant officer from the enforcing authorities (ie HSE or the local authority). Any infringements of relevant legislation may be subject to a formal investigation by the appropriate enforcing authority.

5   There are published guidelines (by PHE, PHW and HPS) for the investigation and management of incidents, clusters, and outbreaks of legionnaires' disease in the community. These are, for England and Wales, *Guidance on the Control and Prevention of Legionnaires' Disease in England*[43] and for Scotland, *Guidelines on Management of Legionella Incidents, Outbreaks and Clusters in the Community.*[44]

6   If a cooling water system has been implicated in an outbreak of legionnaires' disease, emergency disinfection and cleaning of that system must take place as soon as possible, in accordance with the site incident plan.

Appendix 4 Example of sentinel points in a simple hot water system (HWS)

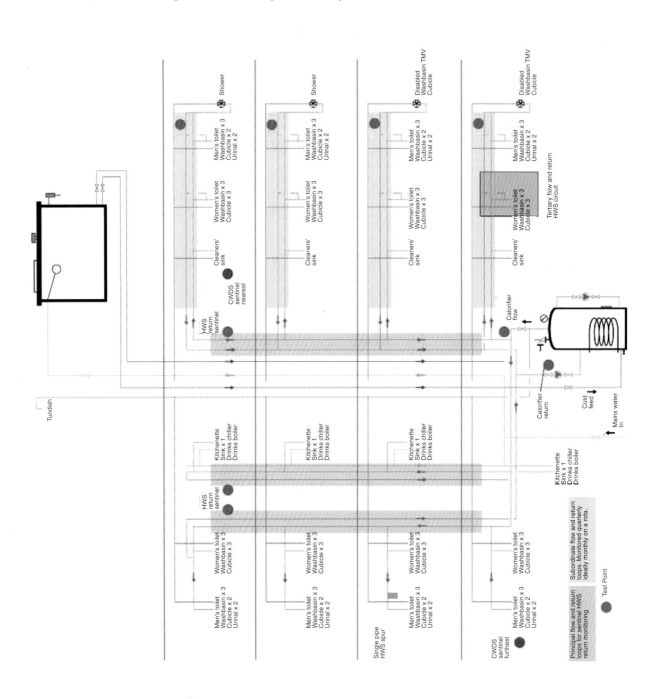

Appendix 5 Example of sentinel points in a complex hot water system (HWS)

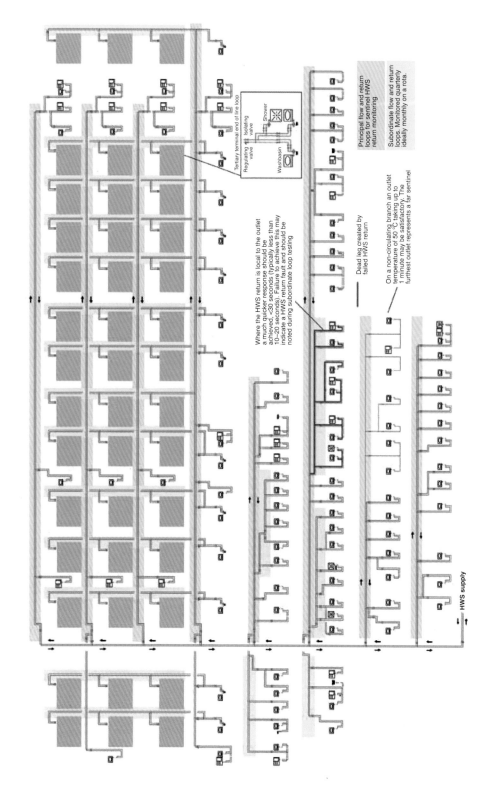

Appendix 6 Checklist for recommended frequency of inspection for other risk systems

System/service	Task	Frequency
Ultrasonic humidifiers/ foggers and water misting systems	If the equipment is fitted with UV lights, check to ensure the effectiveness of the lamp (check to see if within working life) and clean filters	Six monthly or according to manufacturer's instructions
	Ensure automatic purge of residual water is functioning	As part of machinery shut down
	Clean and disinfect all wetted parts	As indicated by risk assessment
	Sampling for legionella	As indicated by risk assessment
Spray humidifiers	Clean and disinfect spray humidifiers and make-up tanks, including all wetted surfaces, descaling as necessary	Six monthly
	Confirm the operation of non-chemical water treatment (if present)	Weekly
Air washers, wet scrubbers, particle and trivial gas scrubbers	Clean and disinfect air washers, wet scrubbers, particle and trivial gas scrubbers and water storage tanks	As indicated by risk assessment
	Apply, monitor, and record the results of the water treatment	As indicated by risk assessment
Water softeners	Clean and disinfect resin and brine tank – check with the manufacturer what chemicals can be used to disinfect resin bed	As recommended by manufacturer
Emergency showers, eyebaths and face-wash fountains	Flush through and purge to drain ensuring three to five times the volume of water in the stagnant zone is drawn off	As indicated by risk assessment, but at least every six months
	Inspect water storage tanks (where fitted)	Monthly
	Clean and disinfect shower heads, nozzles, roses, 'Y' strainers, and water storage tanks (where fitted)	Quarterly, or more frequently, as indicated by the risk assessment

System/service	Task	Frequency
Sprinkler and hose reel systems	When witnessing tests of sprinkler blow-down and hose reels ensure that there is minimum risk of exposure to aerosols	As directed
Spa pools	Detailed HSE/PHE guidance on the management of spa pools is available in *Management of spa pools: Controlling the risks of infection*	
Whirlpool baths	Clean, flush and disinfect air channels Remove, flush and clean jets	As indicated by risk assessment
Horticultural misting systems	Clean and disinfect distribution pipework, spray heads and make-up tanks including all wetted surfaces, descaling as necessary	Quarterly or as indicated by risk assessment
Dental equipment	Drain down, clean, flush and disinfect all system components, pipework and bottles	Twice daily (typically at the start and finish of each working day). Disinfectant contact time as recommended by the manufacturer
	Clean storage bottles, rinse with distilled or Reverse Osmosis (RO) water, drain, and leave inverted overnight	Daily
	Take microbiological measurements – refer to *Decontamination Health Technical Memorandum 01-05: Decontamination in primary care dental practices*[45]	As indicated by risk assessment
Vehicle wash systems	Check and clean filtration systems, collection tanks and interceptor tanks and check treatment system A biocide programme should be in place and should be monitored and controlled similar to the standards required in cooling towers Clean and disinfect system and ensure sludge tanks are emptied	As indicated by risk assessment
	Sample for legionella	Initially to establish that control has been achieved and thereafter quarterly or as indicated by risk assessment

System/service	Task	Frequency
Fountains and water features	Clean and disinfect ponds, spray heads and make-up tanks including all wetted surfaces, descaling as necessary	As indicated by the risk assessment, and depending on condition
Industrial process water systems	Conduct a risk assessment of each system, preferably using an assessment team comprising members knowledgeable in legionella management and control, as well as those familiar with the design and operation of the system. Devise a control scheme based on this risk assessment	Monitoring, inspection, and testing frequencies to be determined as indicated by the risk assessment

References

1 *Legionnaires' disease: The control of legionella bacteria in water systems. Approved Code of Practice* L8 (Fourth edition) HSE Books 2013 www.hse.gov.uk/pubns/books/l8.htm

2 *Health and Safety at Work etc Act 1974* (c 37) The Stationery Office 1974 ISBN 978 0 10 543774 1

3 *Hazardous substances at work: A brief guide to COSHH* Leaflet INDG136(rev5) HSE Books 2012 www.hse.gov.uk/pubns/indg136.htm

4 *The Notification of Cooling Towers and Evaporative Condensers Regulations* 1992 SI 1992/2225 The Stationery Office

5 *Reporting accidents and incidents at work: A brief guide to the Reporting of Injuries, Diseases and Dangerous Occurrences Regulations (RIDDOR)* Leaflet INDG453(rev1) HSE Books 2013 www.hse.gov.uk/pubns/indg453.htm

6 *Consulting workers on health and safety. Safety Representatives and Safety Committees Regulations 1977 (as amended) and Health and Safety (Consultation with Employees) Regulations 1996 (as amended). Approved Codes of Practice and guidance* L146 (Second edition) HSE Books 2012 ISBN 978 0 7176 6461 0 www.hse.gov.uk/pubns/books/l146.htm

7 BS 8580 *Water quality. Risk assessments for Legionella control. Code of practice* British Standards Institution

8 *Guide to risk assessment for water services* The Water Management Society www.wmsoc.org.uk/publication.html

9 *A Recommended Code of Conduct for Service Providers* The Legionella Control Association 2013 www.legionellacontrol.org.uk.

10 *Water Fittings and Materials Directory* Water Regulations Advisory Scheme www.wras.co.uk/Directory

11 BS 6920-2-1+A3 *Suitability of non-metallic products for use in contact with water intended for human consumption with regard to their effect on the quality of the water. Methods of test* British Standards Institution

12 *Respiratory protective equipment at work: A practical guide* HSG53 (Fourth edition) HSE Books 2013 ISBN 978 0 7176 6454 2 www.hse.gov.uk/pubns/books/hsg53.htm

13 BS 7592 *Sampling for legionella bacteria in water systems. Code of practice* British Standards Institution

14 EN ISO/IEC 17025 *General requirements for the competence of testing and calibration laboratories* British Standards Institution

15 BS 6068-4.12, ISO 11731 *Water quality. Microbiological methods. Detection and enumeration of legionella* British Standards Institution

16 *Health and safety in care homes* HSG220 HSE Books 2001
ISBN 978 0 7176 2082 1 www.hse.gov.uk/pubns/books/hsg220.htm

17 *Water systems: Health Technical Memorandum 04–01: The control of Legionella, hygiene, 'safe' hot water, cold water and drinking water systems* Department of Health 2006

18 *Scottish Health Technical Memorandum 04-01* Health Facilities Scotland
www.hfs.scot.nhs.uk/publications-1/engineering/shtm-04-01/

19 *Water Supply (Water Fitting) Regulations* 1999 SI 1148/1999 The Stationery Office

20 *Water Byelaws 2004* Scottish Water www.scottishwater.co.uk

21 BS 3198 *Specification for copper hot water storage combination units for domestic purposes* British Standards Institution

22 *Managing health and safety in construction. Construction (Design and Management) Regulations 2007. Approved Code of Practice* L144 HSE Books 2007 ISBN 978 0 7176 6223 4 www.hse.gov.uk/pubns/books/l144.htm

23 Approved Documents for Building Regulations in England and Wales:
www.planningportal.gov.uk/buildingregulations/
Approved Documents for Building Regulations in Scotland:
www.scotland.gov.uk/Topics/Built-Environment/Building/Building-standards

24 *The Private Water Supplies Regulations 2009* SI 3101/2009
The Stationery Office

25 *The Private Water Supplies (Wales) Regulations 2010* Welsh SI 66/2010
The Stationery Office

26 *The Private Water Supplies (Scotland) Regulations 2006* SSI 209/2006
The Stationery Office

27 BS EN 806 (Parts 1–5) *Specifications for installations inside buildings conveying water for human consumption* British Standards Institution

28 BS 8558 *Guide to the design, installation, testing and maintenance of services supplying water for domestic use within buildings and their curtilages* British Standards Institution

29 *Guide G: Public Health Engineering* CIBSE www.cibse.org

30 *The Water Supply (Water Quality) Regulations 2000* SI 3184/2000
The Stationery Office

31 *Water Industry Act 1991* The Stationery Office 1991 ISBN 978 0 10 545691 9

32 *Water (Scotland) Act 1980* The Stationery Office 1980 ISBN 978 0 10 544580 7

33 *The Water Supply (Water Quality) (Wales) Regulations 2010* SI 994/2010
The Stationery Office

34 *The Water Supply (Water Quality) (Scotland) Regulations 2001* SSI 207/2001
The Stationery Office

35 *The Water Supply (Water Quality) (Scotland) Regulations 2010* SSI 95/2010
The Stationery Office

36 BS EN 12671 *Chemicals used for treatment of water intended for human consumption. Chlorine dioxide generated in situ* British Standards Institution

37 BS 7592 *Sampling for Legionella organisms in water systems. Code of Practice* British Standards Institution

38 *Controlling scalding risks from bathing and showering* United Kingdom Homecare Association (UKHCA) www.ukhca.co.uk

39 *Thermostatic mixing valves (healthcare premises)* NHS Model Engineering Specifications D08 NHS 1997

40 *Management of spa pools: Controlling the risks of infection* HPA/HSE 2006 www.hse.gov.uk/legionnaires/spapools.htm

41 *The Health Protection (Notification) Regulations 2010* SI 659/2010
The Stationery Office

42 *The Public Health (Notification of Infectious Diseases) (Scotland) Regulations 1988* SI 1550/1988 The Stationery Office

43 *Guidance on the Control and Prevention of Legionnaires' Disease in England* Health Protection Agency 2010 www.hpa.org.uk

44 *Guidelines on management of Legionella Incidents, Outbreaks and Clusters in the Community* Health Protection Scotland 2009 www.hpa.scot.nhs.uk

45 *Decontamination Health Technical Memorandum 01-05: Decontamination in primary care dental practices* Department of Health www.gov.uk

Glossary

adiabatic cooler/condenser a term used to describe a heat rejection device that normally operates in dry mode but which can also operate using evaporative cooling to pre-cool the air stream with water, to increase the device's cooling capacity when ambient air temperatures are high, eg in the summer months.

aerosol a suspension in a gaseous medium of solid particles, liquid particles or solid and liquid particles having negligible falling velocity. In the context of this document, it is a suspension of particles which may contain legionella with a typical droplet size of <5 µm that can be inhaled deep into the lungs.

air conditioning a form of air treatment whereby temperature, humidity, ventilation and air cleanliness are controlled within limits determined by the requirements of the air-conditioned enclosure.

acid a chemical that reduces the pH of water and reacts with alkali or base, commonly used for removing scale and other deposits from systems and sometimes used as a scale inhibitor.

algae simple organisms similar to plants that require light for growth, typically found in aquatic environments.

alkali a chemical that increases the pH of water and reacts with an acid.

alkalinity the concentration of alkali in water (measured by titration with standard acid solution).

antibodies substances in the blood that destroy or neutralise toxins or components of bacteria known generally as antigens; and are formed as a result of the introduction into the body of the antigen to which they are antagonistic.

adenosine triphosphate (ATP) a chemical used as an energy source in cells for metabolic purposes. Its concentration in water can be used to estimate microbial population density.

bacterium (plural bacteria) a microscopic, unicellular prokaryotic organism, without a nuclear membrane.

balance pipes pipe(s) between adjoining duty towers and between duty and standby towers.

biocide a substance that kills microorganisms.

biofilm a community of microorganisms of different types growing together on a surface so that they form a slime layer.

bleed a deliberate intermittent or continuous discharge of system water to drain to allow the admission of make-up water to the system, thereby controlling the concentration of dissolved or suspended solids in the water.

blow-down another term for bleed.

bromine an element very similar to chlorine used as a biocide and sometimes as a disinfectant. The main practical difference between bromine and chlorine when used as a biocide is that bromine remains effective at higher pH levels.

calorifier an apparatus used for the transfer of heat to water in a vessel, the source of heat being contained within a pipe or coil immersed in the water.

chlorinate to add chlorine to water, usually in the form of a hypochlorite.

chlorine an element used as a biocide and for disinfection (see also **bromine, combined chlorine** and **free chlorine**).

chlorine dioxide a compound used as a biocide.

cold water service installation of plant, pipes and fitting in which cold water is stored, distributed and subsequently discharged.

combined chlorine the amount of chlorine that has reacted with nitrogenous or organic materials to form chlorine compounds. If the materials are nitrogenous then the compounds formed are chloramines.

concentration factor compares the level of dissolved solids in the cooling water with that dissolved in the make-up water (also known as cycles of concentration or concentration ratio). Usually determined by comparison of either the chloride or magnesium concentration.

conductivity the capacity of the ions in the water to carry electrical current. Conductivity measurement is used to estimate the Total Dissolved Solids (TDS) in the water. The results are expressed as microsiemens/cm (µS/cm) and are temperature dependent. TDS can be calculated by multiplying the conductivity level with a conversion factor of 0.7. Care should be taken not to confuse conductivity and TDS figures (see **TDS**).

conductivity controller a device that measures the electrical conductivity of water and helps control it to a pre-set value.

contact time the time a chemical is retained in the system.

cooling water system a heat exchange system comprising a heat-rejection plant and interconnecting recirculating water pipework (with associated pumps, valves and controls).

corrosion coupons small strips of various types of metal, placed in racks in water circuits, that can easily be removed, weighed and/or inspected to enable the corrosion characteristics of the water to be assessed.

corrosion inhibitors chemicals designed to prevent or slow down the waterside corrosion of metals by: passivating the metal by the promotion of a thin metal oxide film (anodic inhibitors); or physically forming a thin barrier film by controlled deposition (cathodic inhibitors).

culture the technique of detecting and enumerating bacteria by growing on an artificial medium such as agar.

DPD No 1 an indicator used in the colorimetric determination of the concentration of oxidising biocides. DPD No 1 reacts to the presence of strong biocidal species, including free chlorine and total bromine (free and combined).

dead end/blind end a length of pipe closed at one end through which no water passes.

dead leg a length of water system pipework leading to a fitting through which water only passes infrequently when there is draw off from the fitting, providing the potential for stagnation.

dip slide coated plastic slide on which microorganisms can be grown, examined and quantified. They provide a broad indication of microbial growth only.

disinfection the reduction of the number of microorganisms to safe levels by either chemical or non-chemical means (eg biocides, heat or radiation).

dispersant a chemical that loosens organic material, such as biofilm, adhering to surfaces.

distribution circuit pipework which distributes water from hot or cold water plant to one or more fittings/appliances.

domestic water hot and cold water intended for drinking, washing, cooking, food preparation or other domestic purposes.

drift eliminator equipment containing a complex system of baffles designed to minimise drift (see **drift**) discharging from a cooling tower or evaporative condenser.

evaporative cooling the process of evaporating part of a liquid which removes the necessary latent heat of evaporation from the main bulk of the liquid, cooling it.

fouling organic growth or other deposits on heat transfer surfaces causing loss in efficiency.

free chlorine the amount of chlorine available to act as a disinfectant in water. Note that disinfection properties are strongly affected by the pH of the water and decline rapidly in alkaline conditions.

half-life the time taken for the level of a treatment chemical to decrease to half its original value.

halogen a grouping of chemical elements that include bromine and chlorine.

heat exchanger a device for transferring heat between fluids which are not in direct contact with each other.

hot water service installation of plant, pipes and fittings in which water is heated, distributed and subsequently discharged (not including cold water feed tank or cistern), **drift** water droplets and aerosols entrained in the air that discharges from a cooling tower or evaporative condenser. **Note:** The visible plume often seen above cooling towers under cool conditions is likely to be condensing water vapour (evaporated in the cooling process) rather than system water droplets/aerosol carried over.

hypobromite ion (OBr–) a form of bromine predominant at higher pH levels. While it has biocidal properties, it is less effective as a biocide than HOBr.

hypochlorite ion (OCl–) a form of chlorine predominant at higher pH levels. While it has biocidal properties, it is less effective as a biocide than HOCl.

hypobromous acid (HOBr) the form of bromine that is most effective as a biocide.

hypochlorous acid (HOCl) the form of chlorine that is most effective as a biocide.

incubation temperature the temperature dip slides or inoculated culture media should be held at, for long enough for bacterial growth to become evident. The incubation temperature depends on the type of microorganism being tested for in the water sample.

legionnaires' disease a form of pneumonia caused by bacteria of the genus *legionella*.

legionella (plural legionellae) a bacterium (or bacteria) of the genus *legionella*.

Legionella pneumophila a species of bacterium that is the most common cause of legionnaires' disease and Pontiac fever.

legionellosis any illness caused by exposure to legionella.

make-up water fresh water added to a recirculating water system to compensate for losses by evaporation, bleed, drift, windage and leakage.

mg/l (milligrams per litre) a measure of dissolved substances given as the number of parts there are in a million parts of solvent. It is numerically equivalent to ppm (parts per million) with respect to water.

microorganism an organism of microscopic size, including bacteria, fungi and viruses.

neonates newborn children.

nutrient a food source for microorganisms.

pasteurisation heat treatment to destroy microorganisms, usually at high temperature.

pH the logarithm of the reciprocal of the hydrogen ion concentration in water, expressed as a number between 0 and 14 to indicate how acidic or alkaline the water is. Values below 7 are increasingly acidic, 7 is neutral, and values higher than 7 are progressively alkaline. However, acidity and alkalinity are not proportional to pH (see **acidity** and **alkalinity**).

planktonic free-floating microorganisms in an aquatic system.

point of use (POU) filters a filter with a maximal pore size of 0.2 µm applied at the outlet, which removes bacteria from the water flow.

ppm (parts per million) a measure of dissolved substances given as the number of parts there are in a million parts of solvent. It is numerically equivalent to milligrams per litre (mg/l) with respect to water.

risk assessment identifying and assessing the risk from legionellosis from work activities and water sources on premises and determining any necessary precautionary measures.

scale inhibitors chemicals added to water to inhibit scale formation. They function by holding up the precipitation process and/or distorting the crystal shape, thus preventing the build-up of a hard adherent scale.

scaling indices these are predictors for the scale-forming or corrosive properties of water.

sentinel taps for hot water services – the first and last taps on a recirculating system. For cold water systems (or non-recirculating HWS), the nearest and furthest taps from the storage tank. The choice of sentinel taps may also include other taps which represent parts of the recirculating system where monitoring can aid control.

sero-group a sub-group of the main species.

sessile aquatic microorganisms adhering to a surface, normally as part of a biofilm.

shot dose a single dose of a chemical, sometimes called a 'shock' or 'shot' dose. It can also describe routine high concentration periodic dosing (such as with non-oxidising biocides or dispersants) to distinguish it from maintaining a low concentration of chemical continuously.

shunt pump a circulation pump fitted to hot water service/plant to overcome the temperature stratification of the stored water.

slime a mucus-like exudate that covers a surface produced by some microorganisms.

sludge a general term for soft mud-like deposits found on heat transfer surfaces or other important sections of a cooling system. Also found at the base of calorifiers and cold water storage tanks.

stagnation the condition where water ceases to flow and is therefore liable to microbiological growth.

strainers coarse filters usually positioned upstream of a sensitive component, such as a pump control valve or heat exchanger, to protect it from debris.

thermal disinfection heat treatment to disinfect a system.

thermostatic mixing valve a mixing valve in which the temperature at the outlet is pre-selected and controlled automatically by the valve.

total dissolved solids (TDS) the quantity of solids dissolved in the water, measured in mg/l. These solids will typically include calcium and magnesium (sodium in softened water), bicarbonate, chloride, sulphate and traces of other materials. TDS can be measured directly or determined indirectly from the conductivity reading (see **conductivity**).

total viable counts (TVC) the total number of culturable bacteria (per volume or area) in a given sample (does not include legionella).

turbidity the opacity of a liquid, eg cloudiness caused by a suspension of particles.

windage water lost when wind forces an unusual flow pattern through the base of a cooling tower and blows droplets out of the tower.

wholesome water water supplied for such domestic purposes as cooking, drinking, food preparation or washing; or supplied to premises in which food is produced.

Further sources of advice

United Kingdom Accreditation Service (UKAS), 21–47 High Street, Feltham, Middlesex TW13 4UN www.UKAS.com

Public Health England (PHE)
www.gov.uk/government/organisations/public-health-england

Public Health Wales (PHW) www.publichealthwales.wales.nhs.uk

Health Protection Scotland (HPS) www.hps.scot.nhs.uk

Acknowledgements

HSE thanks the following organisations for providing representatives with technical expertise, which was used when preparing the technical guidance that appears in this publication: Legionella Control Association (Howard Barnes, Robert McLeod-Smith); British Association for Chemical Specialities (Tim Parkinson, Geoff Walker, John Smith); Water Management Society (John Lindeman, Alan Elsworth, Mike Hunter, Graham Thompson, Giles Green, Alan Greaves, Susanne Lee); and Dr Tom Makin.

Further information

For information about health and safety, or to report inconsistencies or inaccuracies in this guidance, visit www.hse.gov.uk/. You can view HSE guidance online and order priced publications from the website. HSE priced publications are also available from bookshops.

This guidance is issued by the Health and Safety Executive. Following the guidance is not compulsory, unless specifically stated, and you are free to take other action. But if you do follow the guidance you will normally be doing enough to comply with the law. Health and safety inspectors seek to secure compliance with the law and may refer to this guidance.

The Stationery Office publications are available from The Stationery Office, PO Box 29, Norwich NR3 1GN Tel: 0870 600 5522 Fax: 0870 600 5533 email: customer.services@tso.co.uk Website: www.tsoshop.co.uk/ (They are also available from bookshops.) Statutory Instruments can be viewed free of charge at www.legislation.gov.uk/, where you can also search for changes to legislation.

This guidance is available online at www.hse.gov.uk/pubns/books/hsg274.htm.

Printed and published by the Health and Safety Executive   06/14   HSG274